6 9

The Babel Guide to
Welsh Fiction
by Ray Keenoy, S.Rhian Reynolds
and Sioned Puw Rowlands

with Will Atkins Angharad Brown Fflur Dafydd
Gwen Davies Diarmuid Johnson Sara Penrhyn Jones
Ceridwen Lloyd-Morgan Sarah Morse Claire Powell
Harri Roberts John Rowlands & Gareth Stanton

BOULEVARD

Babel Guide to Welsh Fiction

©Boulevard Books 2009
First Published 2009 by Boulevard Books
71 Lytton Road
Oxford OX4 3NY, UK
Tel 01865 712931
info@babelguides.co.uk
babelguides.co.uk

The publisher acknowledges the financial support of the Welsh
Books Council

ISBN 978-1-899460-51-9

Boulevard Books are distributed in the UK & Europe by Gazelle
Book Services Limited White Cross Mills High Town Lancaster.
LA1 4XS.
Tel: +44(0)152468765 Fax: +44(0)152463232
Email: Sales@gazellebooks.co.uk
and available from Gardners

Cover Design Sion Ilar / Welsh Books Council
Typeset by Studio Europa / page design Sion Ilar
Printed and bound by InType, Wimbledon, London

Preface by Sioned Puw Rowlands
of Wales Literature Exchange/Cyfnewidfa Lên Cymru

The *Babel Guide to Welsh Fiction* is a welcome step towards making the literature of Wales more accessible to readers outside Wales. Wales' best-known literary figures are undoubtedly the poets Dylan Thomas and R.S. Thomas. Dylan Thomas, with his lyrical exuberance and wild lifestyle, has come to represent the fiery spirit of the Welsh: those 'Italians under the rain', that fire in the puritanical belly of Nonconformism. R.S. Thomas is known for his deeply religious poetry but also, controversially, for his determined defence of the Welsh language. Although writing in English, his position was clear: 'Despite our speech, we are not English'.

In this guide you will find the two literatures of Wales side by side: Welsh-language fiction and prose published in English translation since the turn of the twentieth century and a selection of Welsh writing in English. The Welsh literary tradition has been continuous since the sixth century. The Welsh-language books reviewed here are restricted, however, to what has been translated into English and together provide a particular snapshot of Welsh-language literature. What is translated is largely determined by readers' and publishers' expectations; perhaps this guide will unexpectedly reveal to us as much about the desired image of Wales as it will about its literary heritage.

Something which recent Welsh-language and English-language novelists share is a preoccupation with the tension between the 'real' and the 'unreal'. Much new writing in the 1990's in English centred on the capital, Cardiff, borrowing from and expanding the noir genre in intriguing directions. Writing in the Welsh language took this preoccupation with the unreal further, sometimes bordering on the surreal, for example in the work of Mihangel Morgan and Robin Llywelyn. More recently, rural contexts and themes are resurfacing in both languages.

Translation at its best is a democratic act, an essential contribution to an open society and we welcome the *Babel Guide*'s contribution to this dialogue.

Sioned Puw Rowlands

Wales Literature Exchange

Introduction: Intimate Strangers — the story behind the story of the *Welsh Babel Guide* by Ray Keenoy, series editor

Reflections in the Cowley Post Office

Here is a mysterious small nation on our doorstep, infinitely familiar and infinitely disregarded. How strange and how wonderful that its venerable language still survives a train ride away from a global metropolis. Coming upon it very occasionally, in the post office in Cowley for instance on a bilingual advertisement, suddenly one can be plunged into another time and thought-stream altogether, as when the synagogue cantor's Hebrew-Aramaic chant fetches a desert echo to the ears of modern men and women as he calls out three thousand years of tribal continuity, of hand touching shoulder in the crocodile of generations that backs to Father Abraham and Mother Sarah... We know in our hearts that such living tradition is precious, something to discover and re-discover even in the face of the blaring corporate 'now' that relegates all but the instantly sellable to the status of anachronism. Long continuities provide both the foundation and the perspective to live well, humanly, richly in the today. So all praise to the co-islanders who have made the effort and sacrifice to maintain in love that frequently unfashionable but always beautiful maiden Welsh and her laughing brother Welshness, *Cymru am byth*!

Now... a word from our conquerors

It would be good to think that the last conquest of the conquering English who subdued half the planet would be our own arrogance towards other nations and peoples. The Welsh experience as epitomised in the literature presented here provides us with a different slant on many common issues and troubles. Community, rurality, poverty, intellectual elites, urban anomie, structural unemployment and religiosity, to name but some. Arguably, for the English, the Welsh are the most foreign of peoples, living under the eaves as it were of our national home, we manage to absorb no more than a few unthreatening stereotypes of rugby, sentimental singing or conical hats. But this small nation, although often treated as some kind of pet in that unequal partnership called 'England-and-Wales', has miraculously managed to carry into the twenty-first century a distinct culture, language and way of being. A culture with both its own specific re-working of Celtic, Christian and classical tradition and its own appropriation of modernity, these running both in parallel and across England's own myths, culture and modernity so that both England and Wales can be heard through the centuries improvising on and transforming each other's themes and narratives.

Shakespeare and a broken heart

Almost heartbreaking then that contemporary England is so generally dismissive of this neighbour, this cousin of history and geography and that we have been content to let that particular culture and language fade, ignoring the advantages of sharing these islands with other nations that have distinct cultural, geographical and historical heritages, as well as a great deal in common with our own. For Shakespeare, Welsh families, dynastic and otherwise, were as present as for the English in later centuries the troublesome insurrectionary Irish were hard to ignore.

But at last the imperial nation has passed on and from the British caterpillar that ate up half the world there has emerged that butterfly of Englishness prefigured by Blake, William Morris and T.S. Eliot and we start to see the world not imperially but again with a consciousness that strongly draws on its own locality and history. Now we can see that our nearest neighbour is not Nashville, Manhattan or L.A., nor even Paris or wherever the Polish plumbers come from but Wales that gave us King Arthur and Dylan Thomas and has been an ever-distinct mirror and companion on the shared island. England could learn a lot from Wales if it could put aside the snobbery of imperial nations, if it could generally learn to look more often into the less-frequented corners rather than always submit to the Great Noise from across the Atlantic...

Daleks, Borgs and Others

Science fiction peers alarmingly and uninhibitedly into the past and the future. The felicitously awful creation of Terry Nation's Dr Who™ series were the Daleks, trundling robotised monopeds, cranky and cruel, ultimately inspired by the Nazi SS, a gang of authoritarian militarists with little stick-arms jammed in Hitler-salutes. Consistent with this was their catchphrase, their *Auslandspolitik* 'We shall exterminate!' (Being extra-galactic migrants they dispensed with the pronoun 'you', creating a suspicion their EFL was learnt from Kung Fu videos.)

Over at Star Trek™ the most threatening aliens were the 'Borg Continuum', a voracious multiglobal corporation crashing through the universe in cubic hives like gigantesque multi-storey car-parks who ingested other ethnic groups by converting their grey matter with nanobots and attaching router sockets to wi-fi them into the Borgian group mind. Not exterminators as such, their catchphrase was 'Resistance is futile. You will be assimilated'. Think here of the café proprietor put out of business and forced to pump dairyised spume for Starbucks™. Or the ex-bookshop owner clerking in Waterstones™, the cornershop man contemplating the new Tesco Metro™ next door or indeed the Welsh-speaker having to dwell in the foothills of the mighty Anglo-Saxon Continuum.*

All over the world the smaller communities of culture or livelihood are now offered no more than the choice between extermination and assimilation. In twenty-first century Wales the extermination option has lapsed but in twenty-first century Sudan, in Nuba-land and Darfur the Islamist Continuum keeps all its options open while the "People's" Republic of China turns the Tibetans into the filling of a Han sandwich.

If in one moment the English might merely shrug at the question of the survival and future possibilities of Welsh literature, culture and language, in another, the potential collapse of our own national culture's cycle of rediscovery and renewal under the weight of the homogenised global 'product' dominating TV, cinema, pop and, increasingly, press and publishing is radically alarming. To put it simply, in cultural terms England is becoming the new Wales or Tibet.

The *Babel Guides* at five to midnight

The *Babel Guides* series was developed as a bridge for English-speakers to the worlds of literatures written in other languages. Hungarian, Italian, Swedish etc. etc. have passed along its roadway but how curious that it is this institution of a 'foreign relations' nature that now finds the need (with the aid of the Welsh Books Council) to train its gaze on our closest neighbour and oldest partner-nation.

As I write the multiculturalism of the 1970s, a part noble, part nonsensical response to the imperial racism of the Victorian age, is being dismantled after the disaster of the council tax-fuelled bomb academies in the Midlands when generosity to minority cultures was taken up by the extremist xenophobes of radical Islamism. It would be sad, though, if the English didn't arrive at the final and obvious bit of multiculturalism that celebrates the diversity of the nations of the British Isles.

Isn't it time, for instance, that the culture, history and literature of Wales became a part of the National Curriculum in England? How can we devote more attention to Somali or Afro-Caribbean culture (fine and wonderful as they are) than to that of Wales? Now there really is some racism in that old slight and silence.

The alternative to having to listen to Britney Spears' music and read about her hair extensions includes a focus on the world's non-globalised cultures, an interest in the locally-produced — there are certain Welsh writers who sing the bones of their territory, like R.S. Thomas (on a moor 'where the air broke upon me as generously as bread') or Kate Roberts ('A December morning in a basement in the town; the gas light hissing like a snake') — who will become a part of every reader. In the words of the catchphrase of the Babel Continuum: *Welcome to the Farmer's Market of the Mind!* ™

*Duncan Bush, quoted in *Turning Tides* (2004), sees the spread of monoglottal English (only a minority of the Welsh can now use the ancestral language) as 'a linguistic equivalent of AIDS. . . a killer virus spreading universality'

anthologies

Richards, Alun ed.

New Penguin Book of Welsh Short Stories

Here we can find twenty-eight stories by twenty-eight authors sourced from both of the literary languages of Wales.

The anthology should be considered as an addition to rather than a substitute for the original *Penguin Book of Welsh Short Stories*, which was based around an older generation of writers. Only one story is carried over into this more recent volume. The Penguin short story collections of this type represent a continuation of a great tradition of accessible literary culture and thought from Penguin Books, a key educational and mind-broadening instrument in its heyday.

Highlights include a story by that Chekhov of the Welsh sitting-room, Kate Roberts, with her extraordinary sense for objects and places and her frequent demonstration of emotional absence or unexpressed feeling in Welsh lives dominated by practical considerations and the quest for respectability. As her ageing protagonist puts it in 'The Condemned': 'looking back at their life, what had they had? Only a cold unruffled life'.

Rhys Davies' 'Blodwen' is something of a Welsh D.H. Lawrence expedition, about a girl whose 'blood' calls out to a rough mountain lad — 'He was of the Welsh who have not submitted to industrialism, Nonconformity or imitation of the English. He looked as if he had issued from a cave in the mountains...' — rather than to Oswald Vaughan, the solicitor's boy, ever so nice, that her mother would dearly like her to marry, thereby expunging the taint of a coalminer granddad.

In Gwyn Jones' 'A White Birthday' two farmers struggle with 'the unmalignant but unslacking hostility of nature' searching for new lambs in the snow on a cliff-face as the author gives us a sense of folk with sheep-husbandry in their line for generations.

'Oscar' by Gwyn Thomas is a pretty ironic piece about a certain Oscar who 'owns a mountain' and 'drinks a bit of it every night in the pub'. This is a good antidote to the piety of some of the older Welsh-language authors, for here appear the wastrels, the serial imbibers and the kind of young lady 'who has been steadily preached against ever since preaching started, which was a long time ago'. As a rich man Oscar has various employees, including his charmless live-in housekeeper Meg, of whom the narrator tells us 'around her face the time was nearly always night time'. Of novella length, this story carries a convincing reek of decay and decadence in a tatty city set in a polluted landscape. Its larger-than-life characters seem also grubbier and tawdrier than life.

A standard anthology of Welsh writing has to contain some Dylan Thomas and here it is an absolute classic fittingly entitled 'A Story'. This is elemental Dylan celebrating a joyous charabanc outing in his inimitably festive and free language, where perhaps, as in the case of a similarly gifted writer, Osip Mandelstam writing in Russian, the English language is an exciting new toy tossed about enthusiastically, vigorously and without restraint. Mandelstam, similarly influenced by another 'background' tongue (Yiddish) played with Russian prose with astonishing results, for example, in 'The Music of Time'.

In Alun Lewis' 'The Orange Grove' there is an utter contrast in both language and spirit to Dylan, with a report distilled 'from the dust of a hundred villages' of an Empire fracturing around its protagonists, a couple of Welsh servicemen, who are as war-and-empire-and-bullybeef-weary as you could wish for; a story with an ending where empire and empire-builder — Kipling's essential indefatigable soldier — join together in the trackless immemorial rhythms of transhumance. This may be the best and most unsentimental piece about the British Empire in India you will ever come across.

Glyn Jones' 'Wat Pantathro' has an astonishing picture of a town's streets and pavements bedecked with horses as a fair proceeds.

As one soon discovers, reading Kate Roberts, in the Welsh-speaking heartland of north Wales, the quarry was the employer par excellence and Dic Tryfan's 'Good-for-Nothing' is set amongst quarrymen and the harsh realities of their lives. While Caradoc Evans has a dig at Nonconformist piety in 'A Father in Sion', detecting a degree of callousness behind the strict moral façade, in the delicious 'Mecca of the Nation' by D.J. Williams we meet a wonderfully ghastly and calculating boarding house landlady awash with little tricks to increase her revenues from her hapless clients: 'She would be at it all day. . . then late at night making sure that no water-tap or electric light bulb was being wasted'. One of her boarders is the trimmer Dogwell Jones QC who, though rather fearsome on Welsh rights, is also a realist: 'His livelihood, after all, depended on being in favour with little conservative-minded solicitors, as unimaginative as their documents; fearful, colourless jurymen; and as much as anything on being in the good books of icy English judges for whom Wales was nothing more than a place to dine and a breeding ground of liars, offenders and pheasants'. This is a wickedly well-observed picture of some scions of a minor elite.

'A Fine Room To Be Ill In' is by the famous cultural critic Raymond Williams, who shows himself here to be an interesting chronicler of the social atmosphere of middle-class Britain in the post-war period. Islwyn Ffowc Elis' anthologised story is both a glimpse into a writer's life and its struggles and a reflection on the crisis of the Welsh language in the same period.

Editor Alun Richards' 'The Former Miss Merthyr Tydfil' invites us to witness the folkloric recreation of working-class Britain as a sentimentalised lost continent of thankless freaks, while contrasting this 'London NW3' art-gallery version with another view of working-class life in the persona of one of its denizens, the Former Miss herself. Its crafty satire on cultural politics makes it one of the most thought-provoking stories in this collection.

Leslie Norris' 'A House Divided' is a Carmarthenshire pastorale of 'that fertile and timeless place' where one found 'the round flat cakes full of currants that were baked on a thick iron plate directly above the open fire', but this is a rural Eden with a snake in it, a lawyer amazingly enough.

B.L. Coombes' 'Twenty Tons of Coal' is a moving story from 'two miles inside the mountain' to reveal the true price of coal measured in human lives, a price being paid these days in China's unsafe but Party-profitable mines rather than in Wales. This is, however, still a valuable piece both for its well-told detail of mining practice and for setting out the reasons why the inherent danger of the industry was increased by the system of accident compensation and insurance in place before nationalisation.

Emyr Humphreys' 'The Suspect' captures the mood of the 1960s very well in a story of marital infidelity and the small-town way of dealing with it. Dannie Abse's 'Sorry Miss Crouch' is another atmospheric story, but a bulletin from an insouciant childhood rather than a disturbed marriage partnership.

'November Kill' by Ron Berry is from a harsher world where marriages don't last beyond the birth and early years of unfortunate children who then grow up, in this version of things, into awkward and dissatisfied adults living in narrow worlds of beer, mates and dogs. But somehow Berry nevertheless finds human (and canine) heroism in all of that. Jane Edwards' 'Waiting for the Rain to Break' demonstrates a sprightly kind of writing in Welsh, free of its moral-laden traditions as two young girls make their mocking, laughing way round a small town, while Penny Windsor's 'Jennifer's Baby' is a poignant bit of domestic bleakery involving an unemployed man feeling useless and also landed with a rather witless wife. 'Do you remember Jamie?' is by the prolific Eigra Lewis Roberts, who has also recently begun to publish in English. It very sensitively explores a marriage and a woman's heart after a long but frigid relationship, showing insight into how rather different people can end up together. Inside this fairly short piece large themes and large emotions are hinted at as much as demonstrated, in classic short-story style.

Duncan Bush's 'Hopkins' expresses a lovely bit of class/national resentment: 'Like in the army. It's officers and men. They use the same tone, people like him, that same, English voice. And, you can tell, they just love to hear it coming out of their mouths. They know they only got to open their mouths to put you in your place and keep them in theirs'.

Glenda Beagan's 'The Last Thrush' is a poignant little piece about dying but the book ends on an entirely different note with the beautifully funny 'Barbecue' by Catherine Merriman, the Rabelaisian adventure of Jaz and Dai, biker boyos of Wales.

The anthology is a mixture of Welsh- and English-language authors and is a significant showpiece for writing from Wales, but as it was published in 1993 there are several authors here who are not active today. On the other hand what can we understand of this nation and its writers without some historical depth? The collection also contains stories by Geraint Goodwin, Harri Pritchard Jones and Clare Morgan. RK

)) Stumbling up the track in the half-light among the ragged garish gipsies he gradually lost the stiff self-consciousness with which he had first approached them. He was thinking of a page near the beginning of a history book he had studied in the Sixth at school in 1939. About the barbarian migrations in prehistory; the Celts and Iberians, Goths and Vandals and Huns. Once Life had been nothing worth recording beyond the movements of people like these, camels and asses piled with the poor property of their days, panniers, rags, rope, gramm and dhal, lambs and kids too new to walk, barefooted, long-haired people rank with sweat, animals shivering with ticks, old women striving to keep up with the rest of the family. He kept away from the labouring old women, preferring the tall girls who walked under the primitive smooth heads of the camels. Alun Lewis 'The Orange Grove' 145

I'm glad I had my boyhood before the war, before the '39 war, that is. I'm glad I knew the world when it was innocent and golden and that I grew up in a tiny country whose borders had been trampled over so often that they had been meaningless for centuries. My home was in a mining town fast growing derelict, in Wales, and the invincible scrawny grass and scrubby birch trees were beginning to cover the industrial rubbish that lay in heaps about us. Leslie Norris 'A House Divided' 292

I was staying at the time with my uncle and his wife. Although she was my aunt, I never thought of her as anything but the wife of my uncle, partly because he was so big and trumpeting and red-hairy and used to fill every inch of the hot little house like an old buffalo squeezed into an airing cupboard, and partly because she was so small and silk and quick and made no noise at all as she whisked about on padded paws, dusting the china dogs, feeding the buffalo, setting the mousetraps that never caught her; and once she sneaked out of the room, to squeak in a nook or nibble in the hayloft, you forgot she had ever been there.

But there he was, always, a steaming hulk of an uncle, his braces straining like hawsers, crammed behind the counter of the tiny shop at the front of the house, and breathing like a brass band; or guzzling and blustery in the kitchen over his gutsy supper, too big for everything except the great black boats of his boots'. **⟨⟨** Dylan Thomas 'A Story' 121

Curtis, Tony and Meredith, Christopher eds.

Re-imagining Wales: Contemporary Welsh Writing [Literary Review v44n2]

Since there is so little Welsh-language writing available in English we are unusually (for this series) including a book-style publication, a special issue of the American (New Jersey) *Literary Review* entirely dedicated to writers from Wales. Like this *Babel Guide* the collection ranges over both Welsh and English works by Welsh authors, comprising ten short stories or novel extracts, some reproductions of Iwan Bala's art and much poetry.

The fifteen poets represented include Dannie Abse, a major name in his era. Peter Finch's 'Chew My Gum and Think of Rifles' cited below is a wry and witty take on the 'revolutionism' of the late 1960s in a Welsh context while Meic Stephens' short story 'Damage' gives a face and a voice to the 'physical-force' Welsh-language militants who were apt to blow up equipment associated with dams rather than maim and murder folk on buses or in pubs in Palestinian or IRA style. Interestingly, Grahame Davies in the poem 'Rough Guide' nevertheless tries to line up the Welsh experience with that of the Palestinians.

Taking a much broader view, in a quite technical explanation of a particular form of Welsh-language poetry, Sioned Puw Rowlands' concluding essay in this collection gives us a flavour of the still-formal poetry tradition in Wales upheld and celebrated by the famous National Eisteddfod. The other essay here, by Angharad Price, gives a sense of discussions about the present-day precariousness of literature in Welsh and the resultant pressures on its writers, citing Wiliam Owen Roberts' remark that 'writing in Welsh is very much a classic twentieth-century experience. You are writing at the edge of a catastrophe'.

Amongst the prose pieces there is Siân James' 'And Perhaps More' which finds a lonely bachelor farmer in an era when few young women are attracted to hillside rural existence. Harri Pritchard Jones' 'The Stranger' encompasses another rural world, an atmospheric Irish-speaking part of Ireland rather than Wales, where a dutiful grandson listening to 'Mamo' (his grandmother) dreams of 'the warm bar of MacDaid's, the place full of enthusiastic, forgetful talk'. A modestly short extract by one of this collection's editors, Christopher Meredith, from his *Sidereal Time,* reveals a talent for close-up domestic detail, while Catherine Merriman's 'Learning to Speak Klingon' is a witty and concise piece on acculturated Welsh valleys full of unemployment and unease.

Sioned Puw Rowlands' whimsical 'A Fantasy in Memory of the Anglesey Bone Doctors' returns us to a much lighter vision of the country. Active Welsh-English translator and editor Meic Stephens in 'Damage' shines a torch onto the saboteurs of militant Welsh nationalism destroying machinery that will eventually help to flood a valley where Welsh is still spoken.

Also included in the prose extracts are sections from translations of three novels: Mihangel Morgan's *Melog (Melog),* Robin Llywelyn's *O'r Harbwr Gwag i'r Cefnfor Gwyn (From Empty Harbour to White Ocean)* and Wiliam Owen Roberts' *Y Pla (Pestilence),* which are reviewed in full elsewhere in this *Babel Guide.* RK

❱❱ He tried to keep his mind on the minister's words, but they didn't seem to have much connection with his mother. Had his mother ever Lived in the Lord as he seemed to be suggesting? Glyn couldn't see it like that. To his way of thinking, his mother was altogether more earth-bound; had worked hard all her life—and died disappointed. And it was his fault. He was forty years old with no wife and no child so that the farm was blighted, fated to fail.

As far as he was aware, his mother knew nothing of the Romeo and Juliet variety of love, but she was always stressing that love, family love, was essential on a farm to make all the hard work worthwhile. 'Get yourself a nice sweetheart,' she'd beg Glyn over and over. 'And if at first you don't succeed, try, try again'.

When he was young, Glyn had put his back into the quest. But the farm was on an unclassified mountain road, eleven miles from the nearest small town, three from the nearest village, and by that time girls had decent jobs in Building Societies and Estate Agents and didn't want to be farmers' wives. Or at least no one wanted to be his wife. Even twenty years ago he was overweight and nothing of a talker. He'd persevered though, for several years, being everyone's best friend at the Young Farmers' weekly meetings, having a good laugh with all the girls, driving them here and there, buying them drinks, but never able to establish a special relationship with one of them.

'I'm giving up,' he'd announced just after Christmas one year. 'There's only so much fun a person can be doing with'. 'Don't give up,' his mother had begged. 'Please don't give up'. Siân James 'And Perhaps More' 261–2

'What we needed was a great leader in a set of Castro fatigues with a gun. He would have stood on the balcony they'd have erected hastily along the front of City Hall and told us we were worth everything in the world and the enemy, rich with gum and nylons, could go to hell. Imagine that. Strutting up and down Queen Street in our camouflage pants with the crowds roaring. No planes, we wouldn't have planes. Some rusty vans, maybe. And a truck, with a whole crowd of us, singing and dancing on the back.

But it was never like that. We got people who hectored us, with their hands in the till and some fake tongue in their mouths. Not one of them wore a uniform.

I chew my gum and think of rifles.

Then I recall that we are a peace-loving people. If we'd had rifles then, by now, we would have given them up.

Peter Finch 'Chew My Gum and Think of Rifles' 234

It happens inevitably,

like water finding its level:

every time I open a travel book,

I sail past the capital cities, the sights,

and dive straight into the backstreets of the index to find that in France, I'm Breton;

'I'm New Zealand, Maori;

in the USA—depending on which part—

I'm Navajo, Cajun, or Black.

I'm the wandering Welshman. I'm Jewish everywhere.

Except of course in Israel.

There, I'm Palestinian.

It's some kind of complex, I know, that makes me pick this scab on my psyche. I wonder sometimes what it would be like to go to these places

and just enjoy.

No. As I wander the continents of the guidebooks in every chapter's harbour the question is the same:

'Nice city. Now where's the ghetto?' **((**

Grahame Davies (Translated by the author) 'Rough Guide' 227

Jones, Gwyn and Elis, Islwyn Ffowc eds.

Classic Welsh Short Stories

Classic Welsh Short Stories is a collection of twenty–five stories from the twentieth century and includes fifteen stories originally written in English and ten translated from Welsh. There is a striking vitality to these stories, which offer a good insight into Welsh culture and the breadth of its literature.

Traditionally the Welsh story is seen as a tale about the exploits of some colourful character living in an agricultural or mining community. In this vein Rhys Davies' entertaining 'Canute' describes the events when a group of men leave a south Wales valley for London, off to see the England vs. Wales rugby international: 'You had the impression that the place would be denuded of its entire male population, as in some archaic war. . . In black mining valleys, on rustic heights, in market towns and calm villages, myriads of house doors opened during the course of the night and a man issued from an oblong of yellow light, a railway ticket replacing the old spear'. Davies has affectionately set up the men for satire, and later the 'myriads' find themselves in a sorry state. In their deep drunkenness they become 'casualties', and the train station seems like a 'bloody battlefield' with men incapacitated and sick from booze. One character in particular suffers a humiliation which he will never be allowed to forget.

'The Wedding' is by John Gwilym Jones, an author who rejected parochial tendencies in Welsh writing. The influence of the 'stream of consciousness' technique as in Virginia Woolf is apparent as Jones offers us the innermost thoughts of the six main characters taking part in a wedding ceremony. He generates intensity by showing us the inner struggles they endure whilst an important event is ostensibly taking place smoothly. The characters' suffering is partly caused by the clash between their Nonconformist values and their desire for personal freedom. The minister battles with a feeling that he is just a performer as he recounts his role in various services over the years: '"Earth to earth, ashes to ashes," says my voice, and my face unknown to me forms the tearful expression expected of it. "I baptise thee, Peris Wyn," says my voice, and my face involuntarily melts into a smile. "This is my body, this is my blood," says my voice, and I am clothed from head to foot in the essential, traditional gravity'.

This rather bleak story is touching too; the minister also feels pride in his role, and the bride's younger sister muses that this day will be something to remember, and as exciting as finding a double-yolk egg.

Kate Roberts, Wales' foremost short story writer, is represented with a characteristic story, 'Cats at an Auction'. Elen, like many of Roberts' heroines, is a highly sensitive woman who becomes disillusioned with other people. Elen has attended the auction of the possessions of an acquaintance who has died, and as the late Mrs Hughes's furniture goes under the hammer, her former friends criticise the state of her house. Elen feels distaste at the discussion between the women, whilst her friend, Marged, quickly recovers from what has happened at the sale, and tucks into her bread and butter, enjoying the moment. Elen is moved into deciding that, after her own death, her furniture will be kept in storage until it rots, rather than providing fuel for the idle gossip of unkind females. SPJ

)) Mrs Jones turned her head up and looked at the walls and the ceiling as if she was scanning the sky and counting the starts. 'When I die,' she said, 'my house won't be in the state this is in'. The man looked at her through the lower half of his spectacles and grunted a scornful 'Humph'. Elen felt as if someone had put a cold poultice over her heart, a wave of disgust came over her.

'Judas,' said Marged, her teeth clenched. 'The bitch'.

'Hush,' said Elen.

At that moment, Mrs Hughes meant something more to her than the late Mrs Hughes. She came back to life, one of the bunch of women about the chapel, looking at them, smiling, enjoying herself in their company at someone else's auction. And then she dropped out of the bunch like a wheatsheaf out of a stook. **((**
Kate Roberts 'Cats at an Auction' 26

Stephens, Meic ed.

A White Afternoon

A White Afternoon, published in 1998, is a collection of thirty short stories whose vibrancy and range reflect a period in which the short story enjoyed a new vogue. Angharad Jones' 'Dear Mr Atlas' is typical of some of the stories, in that a small event in a person's life takes on a greater magnitude and significance. When Elen trips in front of a builder who has whistled at her as she walks to work, he rushes to see if she is hurt. This moment lends colour to an otherwise drab life, and causes Elen to question the way she feels about her boyfriend, Gronw. That evening she notices how Gronw, a scholar, has shadows under his eyes: 'the kind caused by thousands and thousands of academic paragraphs'. In contrast, the builder — less remote and more virile than her partner — is not repelled by the 'undignified' spectre of her blood seeping from the cut on her knee through her nylon tights.

'One Lettuce Does Not a Salad Make' is similar to Jones' story in that a small event, such as a man's reaction to a salad, can be symbolic of more important issues, and reveal the fault-lines in a relationship. Bethan Evans provides a moving and comic account of a Welsh woman's experience of living in France, and her ill-fated reunion with her boyfriend, Wyn, when he visits from Wales. Her new-found passion for French food contrasts with his disgust towards the unfamiliar, and signifies a widening gulf between them. Wyn is not appeased when their bed collapses during the pair's vigorous lovemaking, and he blames it on the extra weight that Bethan has gained whilst in France. The author shows how tenderness and frustration can coexist, in her description of the morning after an argument: 'Wyn was sleeping like a baby, his arms around the pillow… but the brick wall of the previous evening lay firmly between them. When Wyn opened his eyes and smiled at her, a few bricks fell but when he let loose a deep, resounding burp in her face, they immediately cemented themselves back into place'.

Sioned Puw Rowlands' 'A Fantasy in Memory of the Anglesey Bone Doctors' is a story which stands out in this collection. The title refers to a man, living in Anglesey, who arrived from abroad as a child, and was reputed to be able to set people's bones. The author has taken this historical idea, breaking it into pieces and resetting it into her own fantasy, in much the same way as the bonesetter goes to work on his client's beleaguered body. After her treatment, the protagonist seems like a distorted woman in a Picasso painting: 'In a tock of a tick, Sigrid will be on her way home, her movements a quarter of a way to being inside out. Her bones will be sore, but will be stout enough in their new harmony of fresh angles, leading her to stare at other things, driving her head to poke its tongue into new corners'.

'Tea with the Queen' is another of the collection's more challenging and interesting stories, where Mihangel Morgan characteristically confounds the reader's expectation with surprising twists and turns. In this, the most self-referential of all the stories, the author draws constant attention to the artifice of creative writing. In a passage relevant to the whole collection, the 'queen' of the story explains why she mixes her formal and informal means of address, saying that she enjoys 'screwing' language:

❱❱ '- Because language is an old bitch, an old harridan who likes to be used. She's a witch, and an angel. She's music and din… (she was starting to go into hwyl now)… language is a deceitful old devil. Language is a beneficent spirit. When I woke up this morning I realised that language was in the room with me before I'd even opened my eyes. Language was on my bed, she was in bed with me, she was everywhere… I get the feeling that everything that exists is made of language. I get the feeling sometimes, believe it or not, I get the feeling that I myself am nothing but language — nothing but words and sentences. I shouldn't exist if it were not for language'.

She raised her empty cup to her lips and took a draught of her imaginary tea. ❰❰ 180 SPJ

(Additional review on this important collection)

The collection's title story by Sonia Edwards is as intense and artistic as one would expect from this exceptional author, relating a girl's view of her mother's (second) wedding day, probably not such an unusual mixed-feelings sort of experience these days. Similarly 'Linda's Story' by Aled Islwyn cleverly explores some less-travelled aspects of married life, in this case a woman discovering her husband is gay or bisexual. The focus is on the domestic again in 'Mothers' by Meleri Roberts, a short, sharp shock of a piece that ought to be further anthologised for its perfectly artful dive from the sentimental to the bleak. Aled Lewis Evans' 'Dean and Debs' are a couple of happy Chavs living on 'the Wern estate'. Dear old Debs is only eighteen and about to have her first child. Will Dean stick around? Read here to find out... Martin Davis' 'Water' is a graphic, powerfully written story of civilians inside a civil war, perhaps the Yugoslav one but in any case bringing the sense of localised disaster very close to us. 'The Librarian' (Dyfed Edwards), 'I'm Sorry Joe Rees' (Eleri Llewelyn Morris) and 'Farewell Frank' by Elin Llwyd Morgan all deal with the rougher edges of humanity: madness and alcoholism and how those who live near these scourges cope.

Goronwy Jones' 'Down and Out' is a mini-saga of working-class hedonism but with a very funny interlude of male proletarian and middle-class female Welsh-speakers interacting (or not). The material here is both interesting and amusing. While in an altogether more wistful tone John Emyr's 'Waters of Babylon' demonstrates rather well how a person's cultural inheritance — especially if they're from a minority nation — can so easily be dissipated if not nurtured, the result being a particular kind of sadness and loss.

The stories by Lowri Angharad Evans and Mared Lewis, although set in locales far-away from each other, display a similar mainstream patness alongside their technical accomplishment.

Meleri Wyn James, 'Striptease' is a clever little story with an acute bit of role-reversal.

Twm Miall's ever-so-brief 'Gerald' says as much about the place of culture and language as some very long books indeed. Owain Meredith's 'The Pizza Man' should be marked 'don't read this in a library' as it's irresistibly funny with a wonderfully truthful vulgarity and honesty. God bless him.

The book ends with Siân Prydderch Huws' feminist satire 'Mr. and Mrs. Tiresias' and Wiliam Owen Roberts' 'Foreign Investments', a warming tale for lonely-hearts and internet-daters everywhere... There are also stories here from Dafydd Arthur Jones, Esyllt Nest Roberts, Eirug Wyn, Alun Ffred Jones, Gwenan M. Roberts, Meg Elis, Angharad Price and Robin Llywelyn. RK

❱❱ Everyone's laughing at me and Gwenan's saying, 'And two of us run an evening-class for Welsh-learners, don't we, girls? And Siân's Secretary of the local branch of Plaid Cymru*, aren't you, Siân?'

Siân says nothing but smiles shyly and fidgets with her handbag. No need for her to be nervous, 'cos what about me having to listen to a gang of clever birds like this telling me how they're keeping Welsh alive in Cardiff? Made me feel hellish queasy, they did, 'cos I haven't got a talent for anything apart from playing a fair game of darts or round of snooker, aye, and what's the use of that?

'Christ, girls,' I says, 'I thought I'd done quite well to find a gang of Welsh lads for a bit of fun in Cardiff just like I was home in Caernarfon. I'm just not good enough for the places you go, like'.

'Come on now, Gronw,' says the auburn one, Luned. Gronw? Why the hell's she calling me that? 'Anyone can go to the Urdd**!'

The Urdd, like hell! I've never belonged to the Urdd. But I don't want to say anything 'cos I know Martha Morris has been a member from when she was so high. But she lived up in St. David's Road with the *crachach****, and that's who the Urdd types were in Caernarfon. Children of deacons and teachers and the like. They went in for folk-dancing and daft things like that. Cissies. Can you see the Sgubor Goch lads putting up with that? I remember Miss Jones Welsh giving out some comics to the class. 'Only for the Urdd children,' she said, and John Tŷ Nain and me make faces at each other. And I remember a busload of them leaving the Maes in town for camp in Llangadog and singing songs as they set off 'Down by the riverside', aye? John Tŷ Nain and me chucked stones at the bus as it left but I don't want to upset these birds so I keep my mouth shut. Goronwy Jones 'Down and Out' **❰❰** 108–9

*Plaid Cymru: the Welsh Nationalist party

**Urdd Gobaith Cymru or 'Welsh League of Hope', but usually translated as the 'Welsh League of Youth'. Established in 1922 to give children and young people the chance to learn and socialise through the medium of Welsh.

***crachach: literally 'a scab on a wound' and used as a abusive term for the national elite

Modern Welsh-language fiction in English translation

Davies, E. Tegla

The Master of Pen y Bryn [Gŵr Pen y Bryn]

Subtitled 'A Story from the Period of the Tithe War' (referring to a public campaign, with riotous interludes, in the late nineteenth century against enforced contributions to the Anglican clergy in Wales by its largely Nonconformist non-Anglican population) this is not, however, the dramatic account of rebellion and national struggle one might expect. Rather it is a morality tale centred on the lives of two men, John Williams 'Master of Pen y Bryn' and his adversary, Hughes, and seems to represent a shift from a worldview of rule-book Protestantism and chapel morality to a Romantic view of Natural Beauty and Love as inspiration for redemption and moral regeneration. As Marcus Aurelius put it well before the Christian age: 'overcoming the obstacle to a task becomes the task'. The 'task' here is the overcoming of petty anger and vengefulness and the resultant improvement of the soul or character. But it is not the bleeding Jesus on the cross that inspires the morally improving protagonist Hughes but a vision of romantic and erotic bliss, a lovely scene of young love, the young love that Hughes himself largely missed out on when young.

Edward Tegla Davies (a Wesleyan minister and a prolific essayist), aside from his moral and theological preoccupations, had a clever way with words, on a mature wife for example: 'Jane Williams had been pretty once, and a few solitary traces of that beauty were still etched in some lines of the face, just as a few green branches are left here and there to break the monochrome of the winter landscape'.

There's a wry humour too at local pomposities, especially at the expense of the 'Master of Pen y Bryn' himself, a tenant farmer, a vain fool if ever there was one, who is contrasted with such as the Mathew Thomases (a farm labourer), simple, very poor God-fearers who sit by their grate upon a 'hearthrug' printed HENRY TATE AND SON, SUGAR REFINERS.

Unfortunately for the great 'Master', who launches himself on a career as a beacon of the anti-tithes campaign, he lives in a gossipy goldfish bowl of a place where every piece of maladroit or mischievous behaviour is noted and commented on. However, right on the brink of public shaming (he has in fact betrayed the tithe rebels) he is saved by a vision of love given to the man who judges him — Hughes — and who could easily visit a public reckoning on him. It is a suitably religious kind of denouement, about a conflict between outward and inner rectitude not much in fashion today perhaps, but along the way Davies gives us an interesting picture of the life of farmers in north Wales during this time. There is something of a sub-plot involving lamb-molesting sheepdogs, which, like the moral quandaries of mid-century Wesleyanism, perhaps fails to make us catch fire today. However, without a doubt Davies was an excellent, critical observer of rather circumscribed provincial types, even if he descends to a rather exhortatory tone in the last few chapters. RK

)) The Rev. T. Cefnllech Roberts was one of life's tragic souls. When he was born, Welsh life was full of romance; Wales was awakening to the dawn of her youth, and its light shone on her face. Ministers of the gospel had long fought her battles, till they became heroes in her eyes, bathed in a supernatural aura. At that time, offerings were cast at their feet like the palms at the feet of their Master, and there was great rejoicing when one of them came on a passing visit to the country districts. Many lads were dazzled by this charisma, and longed to enter their world. One of these lads was the one who later became the Rev. T. Cefnllech Roberts. By the time he had joined their ranks the glory had vanished; the minister's glamour had become an actor's royal regalia in the hard light of day.

His parents had never had the honour of giving a minister a night's lodging, and their relationship with him was that of people who gazed at a monarch from afar. They never dared imagine that one of their children could become a minister, but their cup would be overflowing if this should happen. They could not conceive of greater bliss. They respected ministers so much that even a slip of a lad, a lay preacher on trial, would get endless adulation from them when he dropped in for a bite. In return they would get the honour of feeding a lay preacher on trial. This was the atmosphere the Rev. T. Cefnllech Roberts was brought up in, and faith in preachers was kindled in him early; and faith in his country, which seemed to blossom under their ministry. And his ideal was to be a Welsh minister, preaching the eternal gospel in a musical burst of Welsh *hwyl**, and proclaiming the rights of his country amid enthusiasm and hand-clapping and feet-stamping. He tried out his talents a great deal on many congregations of stones and many flocks of sheep on the mountain. In this way he became acquainted, early in his career, with two rather unpleasant types of audience, the immovable and the mindless. The stones gazed stoically and contemptuously at him, and the sheep looked bewildered, as if they could not understand a word.

When he began to preach his soul was on fire, and like every young preacher he thought that before long he could inspire the land with ardour for the pure and the elevated, and that multitudes would throng to the Saviour under his ministry. He mercilessly condemned all manner of sin, thinking that he would only have to condemn and the land would awaken, be afraid, and become converted. It was then he learnt the phrases that became a part of him: that the dawn was rising in Wales, shackles were being cast away, the yoke of oppression was being broken, the mountains were bursting into song, the trees were applauding for joy — in anticipation of this event.

It was to Llanalun that he first went as a minister. In Llanalun, at the beginning of autumn, they had a fair they called Dung Fair, an ancient institution. In the first half of the day they had an animal market and in the second they had fun. People would then indulge frantically in play and dance and drunkenness and fighting. The minister imagined devils sniggering and angels weeping when the fun and games were over when he watched the horde of wayfarers staggering home, and among them an occasional couple who would not get home at all that night.

The Rev. T. Cefnllech Roberts, with the curiosity of a new minister, went to investigate the fair, and he was shocked to the core. He left the place with all the visions of his youth hovering around him, calling him to action; their voices were like a cry from the promised land. And he decided to act, to banish such vanity from the land. The next day he went to his fellow ministers in the area, old men who had lived there a long time. One of them intimated to him, kindly, that it was a great thing to be young... **((** 50–51

*passion, belonging, enthusiasm...

Eames, Marion

Fair Wilderness [Y Rhandir Mwyn]

'Good fences make good neighbours,' said Robert Frost; *Fair Wilderness* demonstrates the truth of this during the emergence of Pennsylvania. From 1682 it was the scene of an extraordinary attempt to create an independent Welsh-speaking Utopia.

Boundary disputes dogged the early Welsh Quaker settlers. Borders were manipulated for electoral advantage. William Penn, the colony's founder, had verbally promised the settlers adjacent plots, but their location was kept from new arrivals. While he had literally promised land, Penn had also offered a Promised Land. Before their departure the pioneers had been assured a role in forming the Welsh Tract's constitution, which protected their language; assumed their autonomy and upheld the right to residence of only Welsh-speaking landowners.

While escape from religious persecution was the immigrants' ostensible motive, Welsh readers of this novel on its publication in 1972 would have agreed with Marion Eames that it was also the search for a political role that drove them to Pennsylvania — something mirrored by events of her own day. The 'Parliament for Wales Campaign' was then gaining ground, fostering readers sympathetic to models of Welsh autonomy.

Failure of course was the colony's outcome. Penn reneged on his promises; the settlers' response was gradual disillusion. Failure also was the fate of the Parliament for Wales Campaign, following the majority rejection of watered-down proposals at the 1979 Referendum. *Fair Wilderness*' preoccupation with disillusion seems far-sighted (although of course the second devolution referendum two decades later eventually established the National Assembly for Wales).

Psychological boundaries are most important when identity is under threat, and this is true for both the religious and the minority-language culture portrayed here. Anxiety about cultural dilution is palpable in this novel. By 1972, fear for the Welsh language's survival was taking hold, though campaigners were still then — enviably — resisting the encroachment of bilingualism. The phrasing here of the first settlers' ambivalence towards the early English immigrants' influence is beautifully dry: the English are 'pleasant enough... completely harmless... dangerous people'.

This novel is supportive of Native American land rights. It couples 'native' attitudes and the wilderness with sexual freedom. The novel's picture of how native place-names were randomly replaced by English is scathing, and was published at the height of the campaign of the Welsh Language Society (Cymdeithas yr Iaith) to paint out English road signs.

While a story of the New World found its first ready readers in Wales, so did a story of the Quakers. Belonging to the same Puritan tradition as Welsh Nonconformism, both shared an emphasis on work, direct communication with God and equality. Many of the 1680s settlers had been persecuted for their faith. Faith in the survival of their language was what drove many Cymdeithas activists to prison.

Quaker plain taste might have been shared by older chapel ministers preaching against vanity in the early 1970s. This novelist, however, sides with the younger generation of her readers. She couples vanity, transgressive in the Quaker world, with the theme of women's repressed sexuality. Lisa's adulterous desire for the free spirit Sion Ifan is sexy stuff. Suspense is maintained towards the end by a masochistic love-triangle between Dorti; her brother, a dead poet, and his widow Lowri.

To borrow the jargon of addiction psychology, masochism is dependency's nasty habit. This novel is refreshingly clued-up on all shades of dependency: social, political and psychological. Dorti, considering the use of slaves hypocritical, describes freedom as 'a pearl beyond price'. The process of gaining autonomy is highlighted by an advance party of the (historical) settler Rowland Ellis' family — his servants — who thrive as pioneers in their own right.

That young members of the Ellis family in America were split by distance from their parents is regarded with the optimism characteristic of *Fair Wilderness*. This community refused to turn in on itself, unlike certain witch-hunting

Puritan settlers a few decades earlier. Though the Welsh Tract failed as a social experiment, Eames still keeps her faith in idealism and a personal independence which will in a future Wales seek political expression. GD

)) When an Englishman speaks of us living together in peace and understanding, what he really means is that others should conform to his standards. Friends, try to understand our point of view. Among us are hundreds of people who speak no English at all. Welsh was the language of their upbringing, Welsh is the language of their homes, Welsh is the language of their prayers. They saw no need to learn English to come here. If you split up these people among strangers, they will wither away like uprooted flowers. As for the rest of us, those of us who are fluent in other languages, why for us, too, the Welsh language, and our own customs are the very essence of our existence. Should the day dawn when the Welsh themselves decide that they want to be swallowed up in a larger state, then, and only then, will you have the right to run your boundaries through their lands. **((** 136

Eames, Marion

The Golden Road [I Hela Cnau]

Two recent events have revived Wales' love–hate relationship with Merseyside. One was Liverpool City Council's apology for the flooding of Tryweryn's Cwm Celyn river valley and its community in 1965 for the sake of the city's water supply. The second was Liverpool's slightly less controversial proposal to stage the National Eisteddfod as part of its European City of Culture programme in 2007.

Marion Eames' *The Golden Road* shows the roots of this symbiotic relationship in the 1860s, when north Walians escaped rural poverty to start a new life on Liverpool's facing shore: Birkenhead. Lancashire mills created Merseyside's wealth — mills fed by American cotton picked by slaves and shipped from its new docks; all this was threatened, however, by the American Civil War, despite some ship-owners continuing the trade with the Confederates using falsely-registered ships.

Welsh migrants spilled into the city: domestic workers like *The Golden Road*'s protagonist Rebecca scattered into wealthy households; others worked in shops or as stone-setters, their living quarters squeezed into a slum area. The area's chapels mushroomed into a formal 'Welsh Connexion', big enough to support a four-day Whit festival.

Migration is Eames' fictional speciality. She is pragmatic and free from that Welsh pathology, *hiraeth* (homesickness). On this novel's publication in 1978, the London Welsh were still probably our biggest external community.

Portrayals of exile, opportunity and guilt would have appealed to the far-flung Welsh in the capital and elsewhere. Although internal exile is not so poignant, when the brain drain of rural youth switched from London to Cardiff during the 1980's, these themes were still current.

Her grandmother's shop in Birkenhead inspired Eames' delightful portrait of Rebecca's grocery. It is a showcase for female independence, as were many such 'Emporia' within male-dominated communities from London to the Valleys. They were also, like today's Asian corner-shops, a visible expression of migrant enterprise.

Yet the superficialities of Rebecca's shop window display points up the dangers of pride and material temptation, as does Rebecca's quest for exotic, forbidden fruit. Rebecca grows from tongue-tied monoglot to a Becky Sharpe (*Vanity Fair*) figure, profiting from the shop-owner Mr Newell's alcoholism, her acceptance by the chapel and her rising attachment to the use of English.

Danny's story also holds a lesson. A Llŷn immigrant who starts as a carpenter, his profits from fitting out privateers establish him as a corner-cutting speculator who keeps his respectable chapel face. However, this is no morality tale inhabited by paper cut-outs. He is Rebecca's love-interest: a risk for the author, considering his sadism and later rape of Rebecca's childhood friend, Emma. Rebecca is a similarly complex character, whose mean spirit towards the neighbourhood's poor is shown up by Mr Newell. The latter, meanwhile, is a (not necessarily latent) paedophile whose sympathetic portrayal raises eyebrows today but Rebecca persuades herself to tolerate him by comparing their relationship with that of Jesus Christ and Mary Magdalene. Eames' fiction shows a fascination with manipulative relationships; despite the apparent dangers Mr Newell poses to Rebecca, she emerges the stronger partner, indeed she inherits the shop. Nell, Rebecca's love-rival, seems a PC-er than thou paragon, but she is actually a sexually repressed bipolar type, consumed by anti-Catholic prejudice. Nell and her friend's hot-and-cold relationship, with its shifting power balances — Rebecca's maid to Nell's cook, Nell's waif to Rebecca's businesswoman — is another example of manipulative dependency. So is the way Rebecca and her friends manipulate Emma's rapist Danny into marrying her.

This denouement is unsatisfying (especially for poor Emma). Another weakness is Mr Newell's shunning of nubile girls — while young Rebecca is actually in residence — in favour of poetry.

Nevertheless, *The Golden Road* is a novel whose excitement about migration's opportunities is infectious. Eames is equally upbeat about opportunity's helpmate, adaptation. The novel closes with Simon, one of Eames' quiet, ethical men who always get the girl. The scene is a cosy Birkenhead hearth. "'You've been walking too far," [she tells Simon.] "You'd better take your shoes off.'" Perhaps it's time for us to forgive Liverpool. GD

)) And then the door was flung open and the owner lumbered in to the shop. His shirt was unbuttoned and his trouser belt unclasped. Drops of whisky from the glass he held in his hand splashed down his coat to join all the other stains. With great difficulty Horace Newell focused his eyes on the visitor, then raised his glass in greeting.

'Thou that to human thought art nourishment....'

He stepped slowly towards her. Susie turned frightened eyes on Rebecca.

'Take no notice of him,' warned Rebecca under her breath, as though referring to a dangerous dog. Susie was backing towards the door.

'Depart not as thy shadow came....'

In the silence that followed, Horace Newell continued to stare drunkenly at Susie Hughes. Then, carefully, he bowed deeply, nearly toppling over. Gathering the rags of his dignity about him, he turned and tottered unsteadily back to the kitchen. **((** 115–116

Eames, Marion

The Secret Room [Y Stafell Ddirgel]

Laughter fills the first few pages of this novel: the laughter of the Dolgellau Hiring Fair of 1672, as the crowds celebrate their new-found freedom to enjoy themselves. Within a few hours the crowd is a frenzied mob, drowning an old crone in the river. The horror of their cruelty, the complaisance and acquiescence of his privileged peers, and his own impotence to resist sets the novel's protagonist, Rowland Ellis, on a dangerous course of self-discovery as he questions what lies beneath the surface of his settled life. 'Far better leave things as they are,' the rector tells Rowland, but change is inevitable. This is the strength of *The Secret Room*: it wears its historical and local knowledge lightly, yet solidly enough for us to participate in the tension and emotion experienced by the characters, faced with painful dilemmas and religious persecution.

The interaction is centred on a gathering of Quakers in the small market town of Dolgellau, north Wales, concentrating on Rowland Ellis' journey from sceptic to believer and the inward and outward struggles that ensue. We see how suspicious society is of difference, and how threatened the authorities feel by those who question, as religious persecution increases.

The narrative is driven by the choices Rowland faces: between his faith and his beloved wife, who wants no part of it; between his faith and his land, which the courts threaten to confiscate and between his faith and his first language, since the English Quakers see Welsh as a barbaric barrier to true communion.

What is the 'Secret Room'? It is a phrase taken from the writings of Morgan Llwyd, a Puritan divine with Quaker sympathies, who wrote, 'Go into the Secret Room, which is the light of God within you'. But if Morgan Llwyd's secret room is that inner spiritual experience which renders external authority null and void, the novel also teems with other subversive secrets. A teenage girl expresses her awareness of her nascent sexuality 'as if she was half-opening a door of a strange disturbing room', and few of the characters seem capable of emotional honesty. The dialogue is one of the novel's strengths, but what is left unsaid between Rowland Ellis and the others holds a more destructive significance. The value of speech itself is subverted in the context of the Quaker meetings, where Ellis learns that silence can lead to meaningful communication. Marion Eames heightens the sense of secrecy and questioning uncertainty using imagery of light and dark, inviting us into the internal lives of her characters, our feelings intensified by a landscape that seems to reflect their thoughts.

The Secret Room is enjoyable and accomplished but its enduring appeal since its publication in 1969 is in its exploration of modern concerns within a credible emotional context, without being anachronistic. It raises questions about civil liberty versus social cohesion and the relation of church and state and about free speech and freedom of conscience versus political consensus; the rights of the individual and the fear of difference and dissent. These issues were relevant in the political ferment of the 1960s in Wales and in the political instability of seventeenth-century Britain, and are still relevant in the global politics of the twenty-first century. AB

)) Suddenly, for an instant the crowd was silent — then as if bidden by some unseen leader, the mob broke into loud cries: 'The witch. Here she is!' — 'To the Wnion* with the witch!'

Yelling, they made way for a cluster of youths who were dragging an old woman behind them. Fear had made her staring eyes round as an owl's. Her wrinkled mouth, open wide in a scream, revealed one yellow fang of a tooth. Her grey hair hung in greasy knots over her shrunken shoulders. Desperately she tried to pull the remnants of her tattered clothing over the exposed flesh of her old body, and a hoot of laughter went up as one of the men tore her shirt apart to reveal her yellow sagging breasts. **((** 5

*The river Wnion runs through Dolgellau

Edwards, Sonia

White Tree [Y Goeden Wen]

White Tree is the English translation of the Welsh-language text *Y Goeden Wen*, translated by the author herself, Sonia Edwards. This is a sophisticated, innovative work that came a close second in the coveted prose medal competition of the National Eisteddfod in 2002, of which the author is a previous winner. As is characteristic of prose works tailor-made for this competition, it is perhaps most aptly defined as a novella and could be read in a single sitting. Which is not to say that its effect is short-lived, for it is the kind of book that lingers long after turning the last page. Its brevity is a testament to the clarity and control of the writing, and it is a guaranteed light and sprightly read, even for the most reluctant.

The White Tree relates the story of Nen (an abbreviation of the name Elen, which in Welsh also connotes, rather appropriately in this context, the word 'nef' — heaven), a troubled young wife who goes missing at the beginning of the novel, and becomes the ghostly presence haunting the text throughout. Despite being the novel's focus, Nen herself is voiceless, denied a narrative of her own — she is composed rather through the narratives of others, her overprotective best friend, Medi, her unfaithful yet doting husband Gari, along with several other loved ones, acquaintances and strangers, offering piecemeal impressions of a genial, generous and sensuous woman. The protagonist's absence creates a curious eeriness that is perfectly in keeping with the novel's melancholic, other-worldly atmosphere, and the devastating consequences of her disappearance on a whole host of different characters are subtly and masterfully revealed.

Nature itself here becomes a kind of voyeur, closely observing Nen as she spirals towards her destiny. Daybreak 'with frost on its breath', 'the fragile June sun', flowers and 'shimmering moths' all become key characters, urging the reader to follow an odd nature trail that holds the key to understanding the events leading up to Nen's disappearance. Although these 'natural' excerpts seem slightly fanciful and indulgent in a body of otherwise succinct prose, it is worth persevering through the poetic flourishes in order to fully appreciate the significance of the 'White Tree' that gives this novel its title. At their best, these prose-poems are deft and resonant, and create a seductive undercurrent in the writing.

White Tree is a dexterous interweaving of narratives by a very capable writer, containing traces throughout of that subtle metrical otherness so often present in Welsh literature-in-translation. Abundant with musicality and rhythm, the lyricism is blunted only in part by graphic sexual detail that could have been left to the imagination. For the most part, however, it is a narrative brimful of sensuous pathos that depicts loss and suffering as well as celebrating female sexuality and where Nen's absence proves the most effective way of evoking the power of her presence. FfD

» Recitation came naturally to her. And she was easy to teach. Didn't sulk if I spoke sharply when she got it wrong. Which she seldom did. And she looked angelic on stage too. We did a fair bit of the eisteddfod circuit. What would she have been then? Eight? Nine, maybe. She won a good few prizes, a lot of them firsts. People loved her. My little angel. 'Yes,' I'd say, 'this is our Elen. My brother's daughter'. So proud of her, I was. As if she were my own child. That's how much I loved her. She spent a lot of her time with me. She was one of four children and didn't get too much attention at home. Not that I blame Ceinwen, mind. She had her work cut out with all of them, what with her sewing and everything. And I loved having Elen. She'd stay overnight often. And we'd have a whale of a time, midnight feasts of chocolate biscuits and the like! The house seemed to wake up when she was in it. Such a little scrap filling such a big place. Such an empty place.... She filled a void deep inside me. 33 **«**

Edwards, Sonia

A White Veil for Tomorrow [Rhwng Noson Wen a Phlygain]

At eighty-three pages, this is a short but very rewarding book that employs poetic prose, where the minister's house is 'chapel-proud and sober' and has a 'beetle-black telephone by the front door'.

As to subject matter, Sonia Edwards plays with eroticism by taking it out of its accustomed and legitimate channels, and at the heart of the book are several tender but difficult loves; one couple in fact are brother and sister, notwithstanding that the relationship is not physically expressed.

The brother is also son to a father who has forgotten, through the curse of Alzheimer's, all but the most babyish of things but somehow still has — in Edwards' vision — the tragic knowledge of his lost knowledge. In the dysfunctional world of *A White Veil for Tomorrow* the sister/loved-one is also damaged goods: a radiant and gentle thirty-year-old whose consciousness is forever trapped in a preternatural mental childhood. These unfortunate circumstances, though, are not the makings of some grim gutter novel of social work and psychoactive medication but are made into an opportunity to redraw the conscious everyday world. This is very beautiful and sensual stuff, but delicate, full of verbal felicity: 'These are the very best mornings, shiny fresh ones and the paint on them not yet dry'.

Perhaps Edwards' game is given away by the citation: 'Isn't it pain that inspires every writer?' Inspiring work indeed and dare one suggest that if Sonia Edwards were a metropolitan writer in a metropolitan language she would be very widely known and appreciated.

Along with the intelligence and quality of her writing there are elements here that seem very Welsh; she loves emotions gone sour and congealed into a stain on present life (as in 'Like the sun itself' where a long-ago infidelity and its fruit daily taunt a husband and crimp a wife's emotions). Here is the same close scent of the confined world that we find in Kate Roberts, even if the out-in-the-open dysfunctional nature of partners and people in Edwards' world is far more contemporary.

A White Veil for Tomorrow has a curious and clever format, a kind of abbreviated episode-novel with the reach of a novel but the succinctness of a short story. The last story of the linked group that makes up the book, 'Between a White Night and Daybreak', pins down and ties together the story Edwards has to tell, leaving us inevitably moved. A great achievement. RK

❱❱ You'll leave the car and walk around a bit. Your mother has mentioned this place so often over the years. The little grey chapel on the slope, the row of tall houses with a dark dignity about them, looking out towards the sea. It'll be like walking in between the pages of a story and getting a buzz out of knowing that it wasn't make-believe after all. Having clambered up the steep slope with its shoulder leaning towards the salty smells of the beach you'll discover the sea for yourself. That will be disappointing; so far away — you won't see much apart from long stretches of sand and a seagull or two like careless gobbets spat between the eyes of the grey pools. You'll breathe in the stillness. This infinite loneliness will open out in front of you, and the vastness will entice you to free your senses. The grey mysticism of this scene says you've been here before. You'll feel the morning cold grip the nape of your neck while the landscape behind you flinches beneath a wet hoar-frost. This will do you good. All this. This waiting. Standing here to stare. You'll be doing the right thing. You wanted to belong.

You won't feel the damp in your shoes until you get back to the car. It's as if the morning itself insists upon clinging to the soles of your feet. You'll feel strangely small, and the day too big around you; your mind will be brimming over with the vastness of the beach. Two, three miles beyond the village you'll take a left turn off the main road. This road will be so narrow in places that there will be no room for two cars to pass each other. You'll be eternally grateful that no other vehicle came towards you. And yet, the loneliness of these places will seem oppressive. The dark, winding, wooded roads. It will seem as though all the secrets of creation have been woven into the hedgerows.

You'll try and begin to remember. Stories. Legends. Directions. An old water-mill. A sharp bend in the road. Past a couple of cottages, a kissing gate and a marsh. You'll arrive too soon somehow. You'll be there before having had time to prepare yourself, your car nosing its way hesitantly like a living thing between the two gateposts at the entrance. There won't be a nameplate. Nothing to give it away. Only the clean, whitewashed walls making the windows of the house appear darker like sunglasses hiding the soul within. This will be Cae Aur. **‹‹** 77–78

Elis, Islwyn Ffowc

Return to Lleifior [Yn Ôl I Leifior]

The central if not always most convincing character of *Return to Lleifior* (which is the sequel to *Shadow of the Sickle [Cysgod y Cryman]* also reviewed here) is the bloody-minded Harri Vaughan, a figure who sums up the concerns of the 1930s generation in Wales. His response to many things is primarily ideological: the Communism of his youth is reduced to doctrinaire Socialism as he approaches his 30s, and his 'punishment' for this is to end up on his knees sobbing for Jesus in the book's somewhat unlikely finale.

Despite the weight in the book of the cardboard-like figure of Harri, who is portrayed as a reformed Toff taken up with the cause of the working man, *Return to Lleifior* captures a certain warmth and intensity of relationship in Wales. Emphasising this perhaps, the main protagonists' ties with the English in the story seem to be infected with loss and alienation. Harri's sister Greta, for example, has become trapped in a marriage with the monstrously arrogant medical consultant Paul, who is a Prince of Snobs. His obnoxiousness reminds us that the Welsh have long been on the frontline of upper-class England's strong notions of its own superiority and it is an eye-opener for English readers to see part of their society from a close-by but hostile vantage point.

The book is written in a highly explicit, populist style that no doubt helps to explain its enormous success, along with *Shadow of the Sickle*, amongst Welsh-speakers — indeed Elis was the first contemporary author to earn a living (via the BBC) through writing in the language. As well as this, apart from some longueurs in the middle of the book, there is wonderful narrative drive and exposition as he marshals his tight pack of characters, a group which is also well-balanced between men and women.

Apart from that gender balance, the sexual politics of this 1956 book (by an ordained Calvinistic Methodist minister) are hard to relate to today: Greta prays 'Jesus Christ, help me forget Karl [her first and 'real' love who was too much a Mr Niceguy to make his move], lest he destroy me. Help me be a good wife, for to be good is to be happy. Make me love Paul, although he is so odious. . . if. . . if. . . that is my duty'.(27). Nevertheless, the evocation of a more old-fashioned philosophy of life is somehow fascinating, if romanticised.

One of the several achievements of *Return to Lleifior* must be that despite all the work Elis required of it: to be a popular novel in Welsh, to demonstrate that a stuffy and strait-laced style wasn't inherent to the language, to articulate his own ideological Christianity and to be a historical work 'summing up' an important period of the twentieth century, it's an entertaining book.

Apart from the calm-before-the-storm at the centre of the book, the writing has to work very hard sometimes as when in a very agit–prop chapter Greta, who is about to liberate herself from Dr Odious her husband, joins Plaid Cymru to simultaneously liberate herself from awful England. Elis went on to write a science–fiction novel (about the Wales of the future) published by the Welsh Nationalist party Plaid Cymru, so the clank of political cogwheels turning shouldn't shock us, even if an important argument is rather clumsily put.

To balance the picture there are some set pieces especially with the highly-conflicted Greta that take the breath away, and perhaps Harri's bloodlessness allows Elis to let rip with the very moving and human character of his sister.

Harri himself is an ideologically complex figure in a supposedly 'simple' farming environment; he is really a 1960s man before his time, creating a cooperative venture in the Welsh hills in the early 1950s. *Return to Lleifior* is an excellent popular novel rather than a literary one and remains full of interest on many aspects of Welsh society, showing, for instance, that even in the late 1940s and early 1950s chapel is the domain only of those 'on the wrong side of fifty'. RK

)) 'Now, Greta, you're married to Paul, and he's an Englishman. As far as I can make out, he's English of the English, the kind that understands only his own class of people. The difference between an Englishman of Paul's type and a Welsh woman like you is not a superficial one. Your attitudes are different from just about everything under the sun. I'm a Welsh Nationalist, as you very well know, Greta. And by and large I'm against marriages between the English and the Welsh. They do great harm to a nation as small as ours — because as a rule, the Welsh who marry into the English soon turn English... He might even love you enough to become a Welshman for your sake, but there's something else preventing him — his belief in the natural superiority of his own nationality and the inferiority of your way of life. If he were to become a Welshman it would only be to degrade himself, even if it were for your sake — that's how he sees it, and you can understand it'. **((** 53

Elis, Islwyn Ffowc

Shadow of the Sickle [Cysgod y Cryman]

This enormously popular novel first appeared in 1953 and heralded a new phase in Welsh-language fiction — a phase of novels featuring a young, confident, even rebellious generation. In 1999 it was voted the best-loved Welsh-language novel of the twentieth century.

It tells the story of Harri Vaughan, the son of a gentrified farmer in central Wales, who is a research student at Bangor and something of a heart–throb. He is engaged to be married to the rather dumb daughter of a well-to-do farmer, and it seems 'a good match' in the eyes of local people. At university, however, Harri is swept off his feet by fellow student Gwylan, a staunch member of the Communist Society, and he is converted to Marxism. This causes a painful rift between him and his family of pious Nonconformists. He declares his enmity towards the conservative values of his father, and brandishes a symbolic sickle above his head. Harri is not content just to preach this new gospel, but wants to live it out as well, so he refuses to live at Lleifior, the family home, and finds lodgings in the house of a council labourer who is on sick leave, and who is tended for by his daughter. Harri's engagement to the wealthy Lisabeth is broken off, and he falls in love with Marged, the down-to-earth daughter sacrificing everything for her sick father. Before Harri leaves university, Gwylan pleads for his love, and tells him that she is relinquishing her Marxist ideas, but he now rejects her and presses on with his new-found political faith.

Interweaved with the main story there are sub-plots, in particular one which deals with Harri's sister, Greta, whose love for a German farmhand is thwarted by the match between her and a rather snobbish and unlikeable English doctor who saves her mother's life, and whom she marries in gratitude. A great deal of irony is also generated by the juxtaposition of Harri and the good-for-nothing farmhands, Wil James and Terence, for as a Marxist, he is theoretically in league with these workers, but instinctively loathes them.

The *Shadow of the Sickle* has a strong story line, and it is no surprise that it translated well to the television screen (two adaptations have been made, both gripping enough to attract a large audience). There are dramatic scenes such as that of Karl, the virtuous German farmhand who secretly loves Greta, being beaten up at the behest of Wil James, and returning home drenched in blood, to be greeted by Greta. Then she smells on his clothes the expensive scent which he bought her as a birthday present, but which was spilt in the scuffle in the woods.

The characters, young and old, Welsh, English and German, bourgeois and working class, intellectual and dim-witted, are well delineated and convincing and capture our emotions. The narrative is strong and implacable and Elis refuses to deliver a fairytale happy ending.

The novel was an instant bestseller, but many readers were disappointed with the sad ending, and clamoured for a sequel. Elis did not relent immediately, however, but wrote a totally different novel which dealt with a middle-aged woman's obsession with a young poet, and this study in sexual frustration was more of a disappointment still. However, after the apparent failure of the second novel, the author went back to the characters of his first, and wooed his readers back with *Return to Lleifior,* which made the story of Harri and his people more palatable. JR

)) 'Kiss me now'.

'I don't want to kiss you'.

'You wanted to once… that night on the pier — '

'You're not the only one who can change, Gwylan'.

'You can't,' said Gwylan, and her voice was low and strange. 'A man can change his mind. But not his body'.

'Don't — ' began Harri. But she was pressing her lips on his. She had leapt upon him and was pushing her breasts against him, her fingers busy in his hair. He tried to push her off, struggling to break free, but in vain. She had the grip of a lioness. She pulled him down onto the bench… She pulled him onto her, wrapped her arms and legs around him like an octopus with its prey… Another minute and he would yield, but he couldn't give in to a woman who had shattered the image he had of her. With one final heave he shook her off and got to his feet, gasping for breath.

'So,' he said… 'The sweet little Communist didn't get her man after all, by fair means or foul. Sorry about your mistake. I admired you, but I didn't love you'. **((** 199–200

Hughes, T. Rowland

Out of their Night [Chwalfa]

Anyone familiar with north Wales will know that it is famous for slate quarries. During the late nineteenth century and first half of the twentieth, the slate was exported all over the world, and the slate roofs provided by Wales are justly admired. But what was the human cost? True, the Penrhyn quarry in Bethesda provided jobs to hundreds, and contributed to the economy, but the quarrymen worked hard in difficult and dangerous conditions for a pittance while the quarry owners lived a life of luxury. Lord Penrhyn lived in Penrhyn

Castle, and there was an unbridgeable gap between him and the quarrymen. To add insult to injury, the workers were Welsh speaking and the masters Englishmen, the workers Nonconformist in religion whilst the masters were Anglicans, the workers Liberal in their political persuasion and the masters Conservatives. A myth (and not an altogether false one) has grown around the north Wales quarrymen — that they were deeply cultured, well versed in theology, philosophy, literature and music and had strong moral principles.

This novel by Hughes appeared in 1946 and takes as its subject the Penrhyn Lock-outs of 1900–03. The author was born and bred in Llanberis, another slate-quarrying village not far from Bethesda and the Penrhyn quarry. Although he'd left the area to follow a career as a BBC radio producer in Cardiff, he began writing novels after contracting multiple sclerosis, and wrote mainly retrospective novels about quarrymen. The novels celebrate the courage of ordinary men and their families, and although hardship is underlined, there is also a great deal of humour interweaved with the basically tragic main theme.

The Welsh title *Chwalfa* literally means 'dispersal', and the story portrays the strike by concentrating on the break-up of one particular family, that of Edward Ifans. The disintegration of a community is mirrored in the disintegration of this family. Of Edward Ifans' four sons Idris travels to south Wales to look for work, Dan becomes a journalist but drowns his sorrows in alcohol, Llew becomes a sailor and Gwyn, the youngest son, and the dearest of them all, dies young after a blackleg's son gives him a beating and throws him into the river.

Going on strike involved sacrifice, and such a long strike was difficult to bear for the bravest folk. Some broke under the strain, unable to bear seeing their family going without the basic necessities of life and went back to work. These blacklegs were called *bradwyr* or 'traitor'. In strong reaction to this trend, the majority of families put a placard in the window saying 'Nid oes bradwr yn y tŷ hwn' ('there is no traitor in this house'). In the case of Edward Ifans' family, the son-in-law, Ifor, returned to work, bringing shame on the whole family.

The novel succeeds in portraying the suffering of a whole community. Hughes knows and understands the social background very well, and there is the stamp of truth on his writing. Although the strike ends in failure, a feeling is conveyed that the faithful few who stood to the bitter end triumphed morally. There is no anger here though and no political points are made. The emphasis is mainly on basic emotions, and for that reason the novel translates well, as its themes are universal, despite being grounded in a very specific historical situation.

Nevertheless T.Rowland Hughes has been criticised for an idealised, sentimental view of the society he sprang from, but *Out of their Night*, although it pays homage to that society, also shows some of the cracks in its foundations. JR

)) That evening Gwyn… was sitting on the river bank fishing for tiddlers with the usual stick, thread, bent pin and worm, when he felt an elbow being dug into his back. Looking up, he saw Will Parry bending menacingly over him…

A small boy named Meurig jumped up.

'You leave Gwyn alone,' he said. 'He's been ill and in his bed'.

'Not too ill to go round with Harry Rags yesterday,' replied Will, pushing the other side and gripping Gwyn by the shoulder…

'Say you're sorry,' he told him.

'For what?'…

'For knocking on our door and shouting "Traitor"'.

'I didn't shout 'Traitor'!… I'm not sorry'.…

'Nor me neither,' put in Meurig, putting down his rod and getting up, his little fists clenched daringly.

Will realised his danger and, rather than stand up to both of them, small as they were, he chose the bully's way out. A moment later Gwyn was hurled over the bank and he fell full length into the river. **((** 203

Hughes, T.Rowland

William Jones [William Jones]

This novel was written in Welsh and is largely set in south Wales. A humorous work, it recounts the story of a north-Walian slate-splitter or quarryman who decides to escape a domestic situation quite devoid of bliss — his wife Liza is a caricature 'bad wife' who dishes up tinned food and spends his money hanging out in the cinema with Ronald Coleman, Gary Cooper et al.

Amidst the Punch-and-Judy of an awful marriage is a fascinating description of the small world of north Wales in the 1930s. Small world seems to translate as 'small-minded' as doughty William Jones explores the naughty world of south Wales, shown as having quite different mores. In fact the south seems gay and libertine to the pious 'Northman': 'As he approached the Workmen's Hall William Jones glared indignantly at a party of youths and young girls who had gathered there before going off on their bicycles down to the sea. He didn't like their bare legs, their low-necks and their riotous merriment'.

Also shown as part of life in south Wales is an underclass dwelling beyond the respectable if poor Nelson Street, where William finds refuge from his wife's carry-on, in Stub Street, described as 'smelly and filthy'. Hughes writes about lives under siege from unemployment in the years of the Great Depression and about a culture of people ready to help each other out.

The kind of Welshness that maintained the language was inevitably tied up with a certain defensiveness, as witnessed by William Jones' recall of childhood holidays in Liverpool: 'They used to stay with Jim Roberts, who kept a little shop there, and their father used to spend most of the week talking with Jim about Llan-y-graig and the quarry, and scowling at every word of English he heard in the shop or on the street'. RK

)) At last he rose from his block, resolved to show Liza who was who and what was what. Feeling thirsty, he thought he would go to the mess-hut for a drink of water, he would also have a word there with old Dafydd Morris the caretaker. There's a character for you said William Jones to himself on his way through the gallery. The old fellow lived by himself on the outskirts of the village and drew a small wage from the quarry authorities for looking after the mess-hut. The members of the mess, too, paid him a penny-per-head weekly. ... his cat (Gwen — Ed.) was his constant companion. He carried her daily to the quarry in a basket under his arm and talked to her incessantly from morning to night. William Jones found him leaning on the handle of his broom and holding forth to the cat, which was sitting on the corner of one of the tables. The old man was very deaf, so had not heard footsteps at the hut door.

"I don't care what you say", were the words which fell on William Jones' ears, "but this world isn't getting better but getting worse. Is it?"

The cat didn't know.

"How many were in the Prayer Meeting Monday night, uh?"

Gwen couldn't remember.

"Well, I will tell you. Ten. Ten over twenty? No, only ten, and two of those don't count. Coming there to play the organ Dick Jones' boy was, and come to open and lock up the chapel Ned Williams had.

And how many were in the Seiat*?"

The cat had lost all interest and was busy licking its paw.

"Listen to me when I am talking to you, now. Asking I was how many were in the Seiat, isn't it? Thirteen and there were our children among those. And here's another question for you. What will become of the chapel in twenty years? Uh? You don't know? I don't know, neither." **((** 48

*a regular religious meeting but not a service

Humphreys, Emyr

A Toy Epic [Y Tri Llais]

Emyr Humphreys' *A Toy Epic*, first published in 1958, is a classic work of twentieth-century Welsh literature, for which the author won the prestigious Hawthornden Prize. There are two versions of the novel: one in Welsh (*Y Tri Llais*) and one in English. In the novel we are presented with three main characters, Albie, Michael and Iorwerth, and the rest of the novel follows their journey through boyhood and adolescence with each boy taking up the story in turn. Through these boys, who grow up in north-east Wales during the 1930s, Humphreys explores the politics of national identity, language, class and religion. Albie is a victim of class and language conflict. Whilst his father desires to speak Welsh at home, and is thoroughly unashamed of being working class, his mother desperately wants Albie to make something of himself. Consequently he listens to the wireless in order to improve his English accent, and shuns Welsh. The tension between Albie's parents' values is subtly portrayed. Father looms large and jolly as he belches without embarrassment, whilst mother coughs discreetly behind her grey gloves, a simple detail that demonstrates the contrast between his robust physicality and her concern with social appearances.

Michael, a rector's son, learns early that it is better to make friends, not enemies, by using a 'false engaging smile' to win over a bully on his first day at school. We experience life as Michael, whether it is the taste of an Oxo™ cube, bought illicitly with a shilling from his mother meant for a school fund, or the bitter taste of shame he experiences as he is found out by his father. After an attempt to gain friendship with other boys backfires, he scribbles a message on the wall above his bed, 'I have no friend in the world'. We are poignantly reminded of a child's need for approval from family and compatriots.

Iorwerth, growing up on a farm, is earnest and religiously devout. His life represents a wholesomeness and naturalness, although he considers himself a 'weak soldier' intellectually, unable to defend his core beliefs against the more sceptical attitudes of his friends. His perspective on life is nostalgic, as seen when he describes his father and paints a picture of a happy hearth:

'...I smile back at him, the kind man who is my shield and my protector, who teaches me new things and reads to me, teaches me rhymes and takes pleasure in me... The thin, kind man who reads so much in the evening while my mother knits on the other side of the fire, like two figures on a Christmas card'.

This scene is presented fixed in time like a childhood memory, or a beautiful photograph, already fading, so that an air of sadness pervades it. This is confirmed when his father grows old and ill. So too dies an old, 'true' Wales, where thinking men worked the land and believed in God.

Although the boys represent different facets of Welsh society, the exploration of these themes does not impinge on Humphreys' deeply compassionate portrayal of his characters. The reader is led to revisit the universalities of growing up: the beautiful intensity of friendship and the darker sides of jealousy, competitiveness and disappointment. We see how the boys make their decisions at various junctures and seal their own fates as each boy's worldview is brought to life in a wonderfully captivating way. SPJ

⟩⟩ Spring is the most mysterious season, they were saying. The trees break into green song. Each leaf opens like a baby's fist and grows towards the sun. Nothing can withstand our growth, today's foot already too big for yesterday's shoe. Observe our steady stretching in the air about us. We grow daily and nightly, and we are plants equipped to draw sustenance from all the elements.

Our heads grow bigger to contain more information. In school our faces among rows of faces each have two ears down which funnels are poured the measured gallons of knowledge. In each face two bright eyes stare out at a map of the world. The mouths in the row of faces are shut until the bell rings and then they open and out in the asphalt yard the singing music of all the released limbs. **⟨⟨** 38

Jones, Harri Pritchard

Corner People

Corner People is a collection of thirteen stories by this doctor, translator and Welsh-language novelist, short-story and script-writer. 'Exit' is the reminiscence of a (rather banal) theatrical career, 'Venturing Forth' the account of a schoolmistress who has dedicated herself to marking and her 'tada' ('dad') — a firm chapel man: 'With tada I could idolise him, love him body and soul, without there being any lust involved'.

'Matinee' is clever and intriguing; an ageing actress is called to witness her experiences with a (deceased) great poet whose biography has been commissioned. She aims to have the pleasure of 'writing' a bit of personal and poetic history all to suit herself and this will be her greatest performance. In fact the poet was 'a creature set apart', definitely not one of the gang and his relationship with the actress was not so wonderful for her. This is a short but very clever essay on reminiscence versus reality ('falsified memory syndrome' anybody?) but intensely sympathetic – as is 'Venturing Forth' to its lonely female protagonist.

'The Vigil' also deals with events that are off-screen but essential to the present, while 'Freedom's Rose' is a little bulletin from the leftist battlegrounds of the early 1970s in the Iberian peninsula. In a clever, emotional way it contrasts more and less radical positions, which often enough, as Pritchard implies, mean being more or less open to using violence for one's political goals.

In 'The Dance' we get a short cameo of an Indian student in Dublin, living the half-life of one who knows his 'real' life is to be lived later in a socially and geographically distant elsewhere. It provides an interesting portrait of a pre-Celtic Tiger Dublin.

'Fool's Paradise' is a fairly graphic description of a homeless girl living in a crude squat. Homeless but also somewhat retarded, this is not a very pretty picture but maybe quite realistic, including the intermittent presence of a man who comes by once a week, tidies her up and then has sex with her.

'The Miracle' is a very wry Christmas story set like several in this collection in Dublin where Pritchard Jones lived and studied for a time. As in 'Fools Paradise', this is not a story for the squeamish. 'Under the White White Snow' is a family saga in ultra-miniature. This is a varied and entertaining collection by a distinctive voice. RK

)) He was a fourth year medical student. It was over three years since he'd been home and that had been to his mother's funeral. He worked hard at his studies, and had succeeded in each examination to date. As there was such a shortage of doctors in his country, and as he had an uncle a High Court Judge in his home state, Sing was certain to end up a respected and prosperous figure within two or three years of his return home. He'd been to college in Madras first before coming to Dublin, studying natural sciences, and trying to master the English language. But his problem of communication with Dublin people was only compounded by his imperfect command of the English language. They had their own small talk, much of it mischievous and frivolous to his way of thinking. The men loved to frequent the pubs and talk endlessly for hours on end about religion and politics, over pints of creamy black drinks. Women were a rare sight in their company, and hardly anyone knew anything about the East. To be fair, he didn't know all that much himself before he came to Europe. He knew about his own society, of course, its traditions, its mores and customs as regards food, and drinking and marriage, the names and attributes of the minor deities.

He'd read many a paperback about his country and people since coming to Ireland, and read a deal about European civilization as well, the gifts of Zeus, the old religion and the new humanism. To his great sorrow, people seemed dumb-struck when he broached these subjects with them. Perhaps they found it difficult to understand him. People, he knew, were loath to invite him home as communication was so difficult, and, who knows, perhaps because they didn't want him to meet their daughters. And neither did he want to marry an Irish girl.

It would be too much of a problem to take her back home, and to teach her how to be an Indian. It wouldn't be fair either to her or to people back there.

Anyway, what came to mind now, as he scratched his belly, was that it was Thursday. That is what had spurred him on to work so hard and so late last night: the thought of going to the Excelsior tonight and dancing passionately and forgetfully to the pulsating rhythms of Roy Clarke and his Rollers — especially that sweaty drummer who'd been a medical student himself once. Most of his compatriots frequented the Excelsior, as did the African, the English and the other foreign students. Between themselves the conversation flowed fairly easily: medical and engineering students talking shop and sex, and the odd nurse or shop assistant adorning the company sometimes. They even had their own pub and their coffee bars, places where it was fairly safe to crack jokes about the Irish and their religion and their old fashioned ways, and where one could buy various prohibited goods. They had no truck with the self-denial and abstemiousness of the Irish, God help them.

By now Sing was walking across Stephen's Green. He'd eaten a light breakfast — he was the cook for the day. How beautiful the flowers in the park were, as the sun and the gentle breeze caressed them; the formal tulips and the entrancing apple blossom. May flowers, and the smell of Mango swamped his mind for a second. He turned out of the park, across the busy corner, alive with traffic, and down Grafton Street — like an eel slithering between the hurrying people, past girl after girl in bouncing summer frocks. How full of pretty girls Grafton Street was in the mornings, like the streets of Madras with the swish of silk saris; the girls there, like here, on their way to offices or colleges. But where did they all hide away at night? Other women took possession of the streets in the near dusk of the city. He reached College Green and, whilst waiting for the policeman to wave him across, met a couple of fellow medical students, each with his academic briefcase, and each wearing a white collar, grey trousers and a tweed jacket. Came the sign, and the company crossed the street, and a section entered through the small door in the great wooden portals, into the front square of the college.

Listening to the lecturer discussing the various types of sputum and their significance, a ray of sunshine came through the window…   –'The Dance' **((**
52–53

Jones, Jennie

Tomos the Islandman [Tomos o Enlli]

A beautifully made and beautifully written bilingual book with woodcuts of fisherfolk life by Kim Atkinson and a very funny introduction by John Rees Jones whose own family lived for generations on Ynys Enlli or Bardsey Island off the Llŷn peninsula of Wales.

It is the memoir of an old islander, Tomos Jones: 'a small, gracious man with the salt of the sea in his voice'. The story is the story of so many places in Europe: the dissolution of a culturally homogenous community.

The memoir itself reminds us of strong and hardy men making a living from the sea, of wonderful home-made bread baked from their own barley and yeast 'with a crust as yellow as a sovereign' and possibly not-so-wonderful boiled dried herring over jacket 'taters but 'eaten from wooden bowls with brass rims'.

Tales of shipwrecks and of bully-beef and brandy gathered by the island scallies, of mad old spinster women hoarding and hiding their money and desperate younger ones like 'Siân... nearly dead from wanting a husband'. This is the authentic voice of an isolated people with a rich and gossipy subculture where folk were delineated into separate male and female cohorts, as in traditional societies generally. As Tomos himself puts it, 'Life was very interesting on Enlli in my time, going to each others' houses, listening to and telling old stories and tales'.

Needless to say ghosts and fairies roamed at will in such a time and place and for old Tomos Jones, interviewed in his eighties for a book first published in 1964, today's powerful slant of scepticism had not yet entered.

The last few chapters of *Tomos the Islandman* are a sort of gazetteer of place-names including 'Ogof Morgan' ('Morgan's Cave') where the legendary pirate supposedly left some loot and certain cliffs where both men and horses fell to their deaths at various times. One of the beauties of Jennie Jones' account of Tomos' memoir is how things there happen in that (to us) wonderfully vague time before clocks or scheduling.

In Tomos' day the islands lived mainly on fish; the proverbially abundant herring that, along with cod, salted or dried, once fed Poor Europe both East and West and sometimes there were also such monsters of the deeps as a nine-foot skate that almost capsized the fisherman's boat (or so his story tells). The forty-six woodcuts are a real treat in themselves. RK

❱❱ Fish were a large part of our food on Enlli. We used to dry herring and 'gwrachod' (wrasse — a rock fish) in the sun, and when they were hard, put them on a line and hang them from the kitchen ceiling to be used when we wanted. Boiled herring or 'gwrachod' like this, on top of jacket potatoes were delicious. I preferred the 'gwrachod'. Wooden bowls with brass rims were what everyone had for eating.

Duwc annwyl! I must tell you how to make 'potes Penradell' (Penradell Broth) — dough made with barley flour, salt and water. Put it into boiling water and boil it on the fire until it becomes like pudding. When it had boiled enough, everyone would be waiting with their wooden bowls. The bowls were called 'hodad'. At the bottom of the bowls we would have bacon fat, and then break pieces of the hot dough into it, and beat it well with wooden spoons.

I remember, once, Wil Huws flying into a rage. He had beaten the dough so hard that there was a hole in his 'hodad'. He was so furious that he threw the bowl and its contents into the farthest corner of the kitchen, and out he ran through the door and refused to eat for days. A new bowl was found for him and he came to himself in his own good time. **❙❙ 35**

Jones, John Gwilym

The Plum Tree and Other Short Prose [Y Goeden Eirin]

Reading these short stories by John Gwilym Jones when they were first published in 1946 must have produced a shock similar to that experienced by the first readers of James Joyce's *Dubliners*. The settings, in a semi-rural, semi-industrial quarrying district in north-west Wales, would be familiar enough, whether from personal experience or from reading the pre-war stories of Kate Roberts. But the modernity of content and form caused considerable discomfort. Like the stories of Joyce (whose influence Jones acknowledged in an interview reproduced here) or Katherine Mansfield, these are not so much narratives of external events as studies of a psychological state or reaction to specific events or circumstances. In the story that provides the title, for example, identical twins, Wil and Sionyn, share as children the same experiences, thoughts and feelings to the extent that they seem to be a single person in two bodies, yet as adults their paths completely diverge. It is only years later that Sionyn realises that his fall out of the plum tree when they were growing up brought about this distance between them.

Although these stories are located within the Welsh-speaking community in which the writer lived for most of his life, they are not purely time- or place-specific, because the focus is on individuals. Each offers a case study of the peculiar ways in which human minds work. John Gwilym Jones' stories make no attempt either to idealise or to satirise individuals or community, though two of his real-life friends, Tomos and Enid, make their appearance in the frame of the story-within-a-story of 'The Stepping Stones'. Nonetheless the cultural world inhabited by his characters is intensely Welsh. Reading them today, a Welsh-speaker may be forcibly struck by how foreign a country the Wales of the mid-twentieth century has become and begin to realise how deep were the differences between Wales and England then, in contrast to today's Anglo-Americanised society where language is often the only defining factor of a Welsh identity that remains. It is ironic to find that even in the 1940s many of John Gwilym Jones' readers complained that his stories were 'too Welsh':

'Your characters have too much Welsh culture, too much Welsh literature in their memory and consciousness for Welsh readers to be able to understand them'.

Fortunately this volume of translations provides not only explanatory notes and an afterword but also the texts of radio broadcasts made by the author, which provide far more help — and fascinating information — to the reader than was available in 1946.

It is tempting, and in fact fruitful, to pick up on some of Jones' comments about Freud or on the social disapproval of any discussion of sexuality, for they invite us to read into his work some reflection of his own psychological identity, especially given his own euphemistic status as a 'confirmed bachelor' at a time when homosexual acts were illegal as well as socially unacceptable. In any case John Gwilym Jones' voice is entirely his own and after sixty years the brilliance and modernity of these stories is still staggering. CL-M

)) My brother Wil and I are twins. We were conceived at exactly the same moment, in the same place, and by the same love and the same desire. Mam ate the same food to give us both strength and felt the same pain while carrying us in her womb; we moved inside her at the same time and were born at the same time. The same hands brought us into the world and we were washed in the same water. We gave our mother the same fright and our father the same pride. We were put in the same cradle and suckled at the same breasts. The same hand rocked us and when we were weaned we ate from the same bowl. We followed each other around the floor like shadows one of the other, and exactly the same person taught us to say Mam and Dad and Sionyn and Wil and Taid and Nain and bread-and-milk and pull-your-trousers-down and now-run-like-hell, and A for apple and B for baby, and who was the man beloved of God, and twice-one-is-two, and rest O wave, flow softly, don't slash against the rocks, and drink this cup for this is my blood, from the New Testament.

But today Wil, my brother, is in Egypt and I am working on the land at Maes Mawr. **((** 34

Jones, R.Gerallt

Triptych [Triptych]

Blow-by-blow terminal cancer narratives are strangely compelling. The subtitle of this novel, 'A portrait, in three parts, of Everyman, 1977', reminds us that death comes to all, and reinforces the uneasy conviction that we ghoulishly enjoy reading of someone else's inevitable journey to the grave. In this instance, the descent seems more dramatic because forty-year-old John Bowen has devoted his life to physical activity. A former international rugby player turned college lecturer in physical education, with a nice little sideline as a radio and television commentator, this classic macho Welshman is peculiarly unprepared for the bad news ineptly delivered by an embarrassed doctor. His first reaction is anger at his fate, and it is anger which seems to sustain him throughout his remaining months of life. His feelings are charted in this tripartite narrative, supposedly his diary, where we follow the progress of his determined but useless battle, from initial shock, to an attempt to live with the situation, to final decline and death in hospital.

The physical details of symptoms and treatment are very few, though enough to raise a shudder at the inadequacies of pain control for the terminally ill in the 1970s. But this gives Bowen's experience a more universal relevance, for the central theme is a man's hopeless struggle against death itself rather than a specific case of cancer. For those of us allergic to all forms of sport, this is a saving grace: the rugby is there only to underline the contrast between the before and after of Bowen's life. The narrative of his struggle with his condition is interwoven with reminiscences, where I catch a subtext of sly social criticism. He has followed the classic path of many Welshmen of his generation — a rural background left behind in favour of college, then marriage to an equally upwardly-mobile miner's daughter from the south, and the gradual shift into membership of the then newish Welsh-speaking Cardiff bourgeoisie of teachers and media people. When he naïvely returns to lick his wounds in the countryside he realises too late a further loss: that in their flight to the city he and his contemporaries have helped to destroy the very communities which they had once been glad to leave. Everything of his old life slips from his grasp and he even becomes more and more detached from his wife and family. His horizons dwindle until his world is reduced to his hospital bed. Death, Geralt Jones reminds us in this absorbing narrative of inevitability, makes self-pitying, if sometimes heroic, egotists of us all, whilst revealing, too late, the banal pointlessness of much our lives.

But the most chilling aspect of this narrative for me is the distance between Bowen and his wife, Sal, and not only because dying is essentially a solitary experience. Flaws in his relationship with Sal are evident from the moment he receives the death sentence from his doctor and decides not to tell her, whilst she herself — seen from his perspective at least — seems extraordinarily blind to his changed behaviour. Rather than bringing a new closeness, pain and death make his relationship with her and the children increasingly irrelevant to him, so the chance for any true understanding is lost for ever. CL-M

❱❱ Oh, I know. I shouldn't be cynical about people's motives. But I'm going to point out, nevertheless, that some of Sal's friends, some of those sharp, pointed women who ran the discussion groups and social service clubs, paid more attention to my existence in one week than they had previously done in eighteen years. And you can see it ticking away behind their eyes. 'John Bowen is dying of cancer'. Curiosity. Pity. It was an interesting, awe-inspiring, fearful fact breaking into the monotony of life. Well, death certainly did that. I don't know what they said to Sal, but a kind of funeral parlour hush descended on the house every time one of them called. The rest of the time, there was even more noise than usual. I think the kids were going out of their way to show that everything was normal, that the shadow of sickness wasn't going to get us down. It was one way of saying that we were — us, the family — impregnable. The place sometimes seemed to be bubbling over with laughter and practical jokes. It was a pretty exhausting business, I must admit, but it was a week during which I felt full of a mad happiness, hedged around by their concerted challenge to fate, during those periods when we were left to ourselves. **((** 114–116

Lewis, Caryl

Martha, Jack and Shanco [Martha, Jac a Sianco]

This is a tight, close-up little drama with rural characters, including the slow Shanco who 'keeps his terrier under his jumper at all times'. Their farmhouse is Graig-ddu ('Black Rock'): 'The orchard came right up behind the house, making it dark and damp; the wallpaper's original light blue a distant memory, since by now it was blackened by smoke'. This is no rural idyll, but Lewis' eye for detail gives us pleasure amidst the squalor and 'unpleasantness' (as those who romanticise rural existence might see it).

Her eye is an eye for humour too: 'As she put the teapot on the table, Jack pulled off his hat and gave it to the pot to wear while it brewed the tea'.

Staccato chapters envision the repetitive, uncomfortable moments of these isolated farming siblings' lives, frying bacon and potatoes, slaughtering turkeys or training sheepdogs. But there is a grand drama unfolding here about marriage and property as in the best Jane Austen.

One commentator (Diarmuid Johnson) sees the story of the three siblings in their hillside farm as a metaphor for Welsh-speaking rural life under threat from both socio-economic change and cultural and linguistic encroachment from English-speakers. If this is the case then the tragedy it outlines is of a population marginalised by the very isolation and poverty that has enabled it to preserve the Welsh language. Visiting the churchyard to lay a Christmas wreath on 'Mami's' grave, Martha the daughter of the family notes, 'There were never any flowers except her flowers on the graves: the three of them were the only family left'.

Poor old Shanco is slow-witted and dependent, Jack is a miser, lured by the pragmatic glamour of (English) Judy from Leeds who would transform Graig-ddu into an acculturated dude ranch. Martha is the only one — as tradition-or, rather, memory-bearer of her 'clan' — in a position to combat elder brother Jack's nihilistic vision: 'There's nothing here, Martha. It's all finished. We're all finished'.

The story of this long slow retreat of an old way on the Welsh hills is expressed in the poignancy of Martha's 'patrilocal' dilemma: if she marries her patient admirer Gwynfor she must move from the old farmstead, leave it to Jack and Judy and Judy's wasteful horses, her crass, petty-bourgeois ways.

Lewis masterfully builds up a sense of foreboding in this tight family scenario, of irreconcilable, deep-seated and long-lived conflict. We only sense that something must happen, that some spark will detonate the gunpowder.

Less obviously, there are mysterious elements in the narrative — huge threatening crows for one — that provide an essential depth, the space for the unresolved and unknown that real writing needs.

Inter alia there is plenty about other animals too, including an amusing account of a sheepdog's intense jealousy and protectiveness for his master: 'Glen would also walk between Jack and Gwen… When they started going out, Glen would bark at her and refuse to settle until she was on her way. After six months or so the dog would let them hold hands but he would walk between them under their clasped hands. He would also sit between them on the settle'.

All in all, this is a graphic and beautifully described portrayal of farm life and of place, a real confrontation with a particular kind of existence. RK

》 His mother was a strong woman in a blue woollen cardigan and flowery apron; she had a tin of mints on the mantelshelf ready for any children who called round. Martha remembered getting one of these once. The sweet had been there so long it was soft. Jack always said those mints were older than he was! She kept a pet duck too, a little black feather boat waddling over the lino and shitting everywhere. **《** 56

Lewis, Saunders

Monica [Monica]

This short novel was the first of only two which Saunders Lewis published, yet he is widely regarded as the doyen of modern Welsh-language writers, not primarily for the novels, but mainly on account of his many plays, poems and a vast output of literary criticism, journalism and political writings. Although his novels may seem like byways, they are nevertheless ground-breaking works, and *Monica* in particular is a milestone in the history of the Welsh-language novel.

When it was published in 1930, it received little acclaim, and was largely reviled by the critics — the main reason being that it dealt with a then taboo subject in Welsh Nonconformist circles, namely the eroticism of romantic love. Wales before the Methodist Revival of the eighteenth century had not been so shy of physical desire. Dafydd ap Gwilym in the fourteenth century had celebrated it, and even the eighteenth-century revivalist Williams of Pantycelyn had discussed it openly, and Saunders Lewis provocatively dedicated his novel to his memory as 'the onelie begetter of this mode of writing'.

The Monica of the novel's title is the daughter of a shopkeeper and his bedridden wife, and as a result of having to tend her sick mother, she leads a lonely life, and develops an obsession with sex. She is infatuated with her sister's fiancé and he sees in her a kindred spirit who inflames him carnally. They marry and leave Cardiff to live in a middle-class suburb of Swansea. Untypical of Welsh-language novels, the story is set in a city in Anglicised and industrialised south Wales. Less typical still, the characters live a superficial life of sexual indulgence, with hardly any cultural, religious or philosophical pretensions. They inhabit a world of fantasy, as if this is the only way they can capture meaning in a nihilistic existence. Monica is a temptress, a *femme fatale* who casts a spell over her husband, who is not slow to succumb.

The fantasy bubble bursts, however, when she becomes pregnant. Bob, her husband, reacts with the words: 'From now on we'll have something to live for', although both of them see this as a double-edged sword. They are unable to face the responsibility of parenthood, and Monica gradually falls into a slovenly state, lying in her own filth, as if to punish her body for losing its physical attraction. When she lies self-loathingly in her bed and hears her husband sawing wood to make a cot, she imagines him making a coffin for her.

Denied sex, Bob spends a night with a prostitute, and Monica finds out one day that he is suffering from syphilis. The novel makes no attempt to 'save' the pair from their inevitable fate.

Despite its subject matter, this novel is totally un-pornographic, although it was said that its early readers felt the need to hide the book under their mattresses away from prying eyes. In fact Lewis had a philosophical argument to make. The story is crisply narrated without longwindedness. The author lets the underlying meaning speak for itself. He doesn't explicitly condemn Monica or her husband on moral grounds. They are portrayed objectively, and each reader has to interpret the novel for himself. It has been compared to both Flaubert's *Madame Bovary* and Mauriac's *Thérèse Desqueyroux*. The authors of all three novels did not condemn their eponymous heroines, despite their apparent 'immorality'.

Monica is in many ways an existentialist novel, possibly, as Bruce Griffiths has suggested, one of the earliest in any language. Once Monica realises that her indulgences were merely escapism, she stares into the void of meaninglessness. 'By what discipline had she learned at last to deny herself the vacuous fantasies that had been a veil between her and the nothingness of existence?'

To fully appreciate the novel, it should be remembered that Saunders Lewis was a Catholic, a traditionalist and a conservative, a politician with a purpose, and one of the founding fathers of Welsh nationalism. Albeit one would not guess any of these things from reading *Monica*! JR

)) He pulled the bedclothes off her. The feather mattress had sunk into a hollow in its middle and the edges were sticking up uncomfortably all round her. Crumbs and bits of food had accumulated thickly under her hips and feet. The bedsheet and pillow were grimy and torn. They, and her nightdress, too, were sticky with fat. There were vomit stains on the blankets and on the rug at the foot of the bed. Her legs had turned a dark colour and were swollen, and there were sweaty patches under her chin and on her neck and breasts. Monica lay, heavy and motionless, in the midst of the stench.

Bob looked round at the room. There was nothing that had not been defiled.

'Monica, there's an awful smell in here. You had a rule once that the cats were never allowed into this room. Can't you at least stop them making a mess?'

'I've got to have some company, haven't I? If you don't want them to make a mess, put a box in the corner with soil and ashes in it. I can't do without the cats now'. **((** 58–59

Llywelyn, Robin

Big Grey Water [Y Dŵr Mawr Llwyd]

A reviewer should not read too much from biography into a writer's work but irresistibly for someone who visited it at an impressionable age (both physically and televisually through the cult TV series 'The Prisoner') the fact that Llywelyn is the manager of Portmeirion, an unusual Italianate fantasy-village constructed by an eccentric architect in mid-Wales seems to explain his comfort with the surreal in his work. In this collection of twelve stories (two of which have not been reviewed as only a partial advance copy was available before publication) things veer between comic and sinister. Llywelyn is seen as a near-revolutionary force in Welsh writing, and his novels, with elements of both fantasy and shock-tactics have caused a rumble in Wales and beyond. Two of these, *Seren Wen ar Gefndir Gwyn* and *O'r Harbwr Gwag i'r Cefnfor Gwyn*, have also been published in English as *White Star* and *From Empty Harbour to White Ocean* (see this *Babel Guide*).

Of the short stories here 'Ifan is no Turkey' is essentially comic, centred on the unpopular Ifan Llwyd Ifan, keeper of the Alarm Clock Shop whose co-villagers 'teach their children to push sheep droppings through his letterbox'.

This is a very ironic, perhaps hostile, vision of communal life where Ifan is not the only local nuisance; there's also Alwyn Galwyn for instance: 'While observing discretion, other members of the committee felt that it was perhaps time to have Alwyn Galwyn swallow a bucketful of quick-drying cement and give up his seat to somebody more sensible'.

Also here are the poetic 'Surging Sea' and 'Morris Wind and Ifan Rain', a story that charmingly personifies the Elements: 'Not he that blasted the woods last night and stole the leaves', as in a children's book. This is curious, inventive writing culminating in a hilarious ending that seems to be a comment on the domestication and containment that so often eventually befalls macho Ruff Tuff Creampuffs at the kindly hand of woman.

A pure and funny piss-take of a story, 'Reptiles Welcome', has an armadillo, Belinda, who wants to stay in a hotel for reptiles, under the impression she is a reptile:

'"May I have a glass of water, please?" I said, "I'm not feeling very well."

I was given that much and I got to sit down for a minute too, and when I had drunk a mouthful or two I came around and managed to explain the situation to the owner, and he thawed a bit and started to be really nice.

"Will you drink a pint?" he said. "Come on, I'm an alcoholic."

"Well, OK," I said, "twist my arm."

I wanted to make a good impression on him, pretend I knew all about it and so on. So I tried laughing, threw inhibition to the wind, and swaggered up to the bar, but it's difficult to laugh with a little armadillo's mouth like mine, and it's difficult to swagger with a shell on your back and legs six inches long. Anyway, I took a liking to the beer, Felinfoel if I remember correctly. And we soon put a couple of pints away, and another couple soon followed — you know how it is — and by the time the locals came in later the two of us were dancing on the pool table. No no, nothing gay or anything, I'm a female armadillo, Belinda's the name'.

There is a lovely vein of satire here of everyday conversation and situations just twisted a little to make them funny. In 'Reptiles Welcome', for instance, a red squirrel complains about those awful immigrants ruining the country: the greys.

'The Scratching at the Window' is something rather different, a look into the nightmares of an Argentinean 'Dirty Warrior', a man who, in a realistic touch, to assure his promotion takes on the job of assassinating political captives by tossing them out of aeroplanes, as practised in the 1970s in the land of Tango and Torture. It's unpleasant but gripping.

The title piece 'Big Grey Water' is a convincing story that might be about global warming and sea-level rise or might be more about a choking, drowning and claustrophobic inner sea, or about both. It leaves quite an impression as one of the most artistically achieved stories here.

'A Contribution to the Biography of the Right Reverend Brother Stotig Isgis' is a satirical hagiography of an ancient Welsh saint. Like Llywelyn's general vein of writing, it's a mixture of child-like jokes and a satisfyingly adult level of acid social commentary. RK

)) 'My son,' said Ulbig one evening as the two vied for position by the stove. 'I've considered long and hard your request for permission to be ordained in the orders of religion, and I find myself in concord and in agreement with you. Alas, the sleepless nights I have spent tossing and turning this harrowing decision in my mind! Bless you my son, you may go to sea on Hugh Pugh's. . . no, that was your brother. . . o, yeah: you may become a monk straight away and live like a crab without a woman, you may leave immediately without further ado, you weird little sod! But, of course, first of all you must do your military service'.

His father's influence on our saint has been acknowledged by all, save a handful of self-styled 'scholars'. Their brains are small as an ant's egg split in two (the egg, not the ant), and so their claims are incorrect. Years after I had come to know and love him as a father, once in the middle of dinner, he honoured me with one of his rare yet oh so precious confessions. A tear or two ran from his eyes and his lip shook three times. 'I never filled my father's stockings,' he said. 'Actually, he was buried in his stocking feet. He was a very illiterate man. He never quite managed to learn the Lord's Prayer. His own particular version springs to mind: 'Our Father, it's hard in heaven, hello what's his name. Thai prawns well done, I'm still half-dead with thirst. . . ' More quick tears filled the old saint's eye as he remembered his father's prayer. **((**

from 'A Contribution to the Biography of the Right Reverend Brother Stotig Isgis'

Llywelyn, Robin

From Empty Harbour to White Ocean [O'r Harbwr Gwag i'r Cefnfor Gwyn]

Robin Llywelyn's second novel speaks with a voice both homely and profoundly alien. The characters, whether at home or in exile, are detached from their roots and yet carry them with them, like it or not. Gregor Marini, a trainee architect with no prospects, is sacked from his job as wine waiter in a posh hotel so decides to leave his middle-class girlfriend, Alice, and take his chance as an illegal immigrant to the country across the sea. There, in a dangerous city dominated by a Kafkaesque bureaucracy, he meets a rag-bag of characters. Some with Welsh nicknames, others with names that would be at home anywhere in Europe, they include the sly beggar, Llygad Bwyd, a slipshod landlady and her sinister bully of a son, Adam Laban.

Armed with false papers, Gregor finds a job as assistant to the Du Traheus, a character filched from a medieval Welsh story. Now turned municipal librarian, he guards his subterranean kingdom of endless bookshelves where the cobwebs are thick enough to engulf a man. Gregor's new boss is originally from the country across the border, a country whose traditional way of life is threatened by its aggressive neighbour. Ethnic cleansing and economic collapse have left only the old to keep alive the time-honoured songs and stories that will surely die with them. Armed with a folktale collector's pass provided by the Du Traheus, Gregor embarks on his dangerous journey across the border. There he meets Iwerydd, a girl he has already met in dreams. How he wins, loses and is finally reunited with her, after sailing back to his own native land and then further still across the ocean, occupies the rest of the book.

This beautifully constructed novel has great poetic intensity yet remains extraordinarily readable. The narrative style moves smoothly from direct, simple narrative to lively and colloquial dialogue and then to a more dream-like, reflective mode. Sometimes there are clear echoes of folktales, and those familiar with Welsh literature will sometimes smugly recognise names or references. Nevertheless, this is still a very modern, very urban narrative. It mourns angrily the wanton destruction of a traditional rural way of life and satirises its false reinvention by ignorant foreigners making money out of what they now peddle as quaint history (shades of the Welsh 'heritage industry'!). But we all have to live in today's world, and only the big city can offer Gregor and Iwerydd a secure future.

From Empty Harbour to White Ocean was originally published in 1994 against the background of the Balkan war and echoed events being reported daily in the media. Today the book seems to have found new resonances: arenas of conflict change, but oppressive governments, military aggression, ethnic cleansing, rural collapse and refugee flows are still with us. And people like Gregor and Iwerydd still struggle to survive and be happy in the face of such difficulties. The harsher realities of modern life and the contrasting ideals of individuals are finely balanced in a book that is hard to categorise, with its elements of fantasy and traditional tale, of satire, and of urban noir. Somehow Llywelyn has succeeded in bringing together these different strands to create a compelling narrative. At times uncomfortably dark it somehow retains a thread of hope and optimism. CL-M

)) Gregor found it hard to get drunk; he was too tired. He wasn't enthralled by Llygad Bwyd's life history either. In fact he didn't listen. Perhaps he should have. He went for a piss and by the time he got back the tramp was in bed. Gregor laid his head on a wad of papers and tried to pull some loose broadsheets across his body. He fell into dreams almost before he was asleep. The ground's cold bite only hurt when he woke — maybe two or three times during the night. While he slept he was walking Cae'r Dibyn sheep-walks above the old town looking for a path down. The whitewashed houses of the port rise in steps from the granite quay. In the windows he sees grey faces like old photographs peering at him from an album. Roof tiles rise above laurel leaves. A white gravel drive scrunches under foot as the house turns the corner. Alice's face is in the window, half-obscured by her breath on the glass. He walks back down the drive, down the road past the photograph faces. A cloud splits open spilling sunlight on the rooftops. **((** 17

Llywelyn, Robin

White Star [Seren Wen ar Gefndir Gwyn]

White Star is a political allegory set in the future. The Welsh title (which translates as 'White Star on a White Background') is an allusion to the flag — ironic and apolitical — adopted by the embryonic state of Llawr Gwlad ('Lowland') as it emerges from a period of occupation and cultural humiliation.

In the book, the alien forces of the great Gwlad Alltud ('Land of Exile') see their supremacy challenged by an alliance of the lesser provinces. These include Tir Bach ('Little Land'), Haf heb Haul ('Sunless Summer'), Gaeaf Mawr ('Great Winter'), names which reflect the geopolitical climate of the age.

Both the provinces and Robin Llywelyn's novel are peopled with exotic and often diabolical characters. Tir Bach is ruled by the amorphous Llwch Dan Draed ('Dust Under Foot'), a typically Llywelynesque persona who occupies the space of an idea rather than the confines of a character. Gwlad Alltud is home to the dreaded Fischermädchen and her henchman Rawsman whose seat of power is the dark Castle Entwürdigung: to its cold halls wayward and subservient subjects may expect to be summoned, some never to reappear.

Living in the shadows of Gwlad Alltud and Castle Entwürdigung, the people of Llawr Gwlad dream of personal emancipation and of the liberation of their homeland. One of them, the book's main protagonist Gwern Esgus, flees to escape imprisonment and is subsequently given the task of planning an insurrection whose aim is to overcome and evict the occupying forces. But the authorities, alerted to Gwern's disappearance, and aware of his leanings, move swiftly to intern his beloved Anwes Bach y Galon and the couple's young son.

White Star takes the reader on a tour of the allied lands as Gwern travels from court to court and from leader to leader to galvanise support for the imminent push to end Gwlad Alltud's domination in the region. On the way he meets colourful and unlikely characters in places thinly veiled as being other than Brittany and Ireland.

But the diplomatic adventures Gwern enjoys on his odyssey cannot distract him indefinitely from the gravity of the situation. War there shall be and his wife and son, imprisoned, must be helped. The price to be paid for precipitating a new dawn shall once again involve personal sacrifice and, having succeeded in infiltrating Castle Entwürdigung, Gwern meets ultimately with betrayal and death.

White Star is a modern book in the sense that it is highly relevant to times when totalitarian powers have threatened the existence of disparate cultures. Some critics have been drawn to interpret it as a condemnation of neo-imperialism, whether on European or Middle-Eastern shores.

When published in 1992, *White Star* helped Welsh prose emerge from a period of lethargy. Writing in the language had run the course of its involvement in the modernist movement. Here was a new departure, a work in Welsh issuing from the Celtic tradition, and rich in the pre-Cartesian colours of the *Mabinogi* and story-telling traditions of Wales, Ireland and Brittany.

In it Robin Llywelyn tempered a highly original idiom which serves to transport the reader into a world whose geography is the reflection of states of mind, a world without cliché where much is suggested but in which the reader must find his or her own *terra cognita*. This idiom is as essential to Llywelyn's work as metre and rhyme are to certain forms of poetry. It is a fusion of the spoken Welsh of Eifionydd* in north Wales with literary registers both modern and medieval. Through it, and by way of the synthesis of many other heterogeneous elements, the author succeeds in luring the Welsh reader into his strange yet credible world. DJ

*Eifionydd: an area in north-west Wales covering the eastern part of the Llŷn peninsula from Porthmadog to just east of Pwllheli

)) 'It's a lovely day, Summer Willow,' I said. 'These birds are quite something, aren't they? Would you like a drop of bilberry spirits?' And I fished out the bottle that I'd kept from the night before and uncorked it.

She came to sit beside me by the bank and that's where we were drinking bilberry spirits and chatting about Lowland and Small Country and about everything under the sun. Then I put my arm around her waist and felt her warm and soft under her shirt. She rested her head on my shoulder as if she was terribly tired.

'You're so pretty, Summer Willow,' I said in her ear as I bent to kiss her. Her lips were warm and yielding and her fragrance of blossoms filled my head but as the sun caressed my nape, and the green grass under us soothed us and I closed my eyes and enveloped myself in her warmth, my mind opened towards you and as we lay together I could hear the whirling of the warm insects and could see before me the emerald grass choking the path to Helen's Stone as swallows darted overhead and I could see the dry moss on the river stones. The river was only a bright trickle like water snaking down a plug hole and I could feel the sun's heat baking the stones of the orchard walls and see a dragonfly zig-zagging on his whirling wings like a helicopter. You were hanging out sheets to dry in the garden, with the boy at your feet playing with the pegs. He pointed at me and made a gurgling noise in his throat and you turned to look as I walked up the path.

'You shouldn't have come,' you said. 'They'll know that you've been. Hey, Calonnog! Spit that out this minute!'

'I miss your caress. . . '

'You can't miss something you've never had'.

'Will you give me a bit of your heart to take with me? It would shelter me from the storm where I have to be. It's not much to ask of you. . . '

'You could have had my whole heart, Gwern, but now I know you'd only spoil it. The wound is only beginning to heal from the last time; things are different now. My heart belongs to the boy now, Gwern. You know that, don't you, and I'm sorry I can't give you my all any more'.

I felt the world getting colder and I raised my head and heard the arched water plunge hard into the spring pool and saw a little cloud swallow the sun as Summer Willow opened her eyes and raised her head to see. A sharp breeze was blowing, the Flame Birds had long since vanished from the trees and the evening dew was deep and menacing on the bowed blades of the green grass.

'Damn that cloud,' she said nestling closer.

A long time passed and the ground grew cold.

'Best not to mention I've been up here with you, drinking and so on. . . '. I said but I couldn't keep my voice from grating.

'Why then?' she said looking puzzled.

'Listen, Summer Willow, just in case you've got the wrong idea, I only came up here to keep you company; it must be lonely up here drawing water by yourself all day. The spirits went straight to my head. . . '.

All she did was jump angrily to her feet, straighten her skirts, snatch her pitcher and stride away from me with her bare feet slapping like flatfish on the smooth stones. **((** 23–24

Morgan, Mihangel

Melog [Melog]

A mysterious young foreigner, Melog, intrudes into the life of a retiring academic in a small place in the Welsh valleys. Using a moderately playful literary format (with many references to actual and imagined books from the Welsh and European past creating a puzzle-book pleasure) there is also an extended Sci-Fi metaphor for the relationship between England and Wales or between other unequal partnerships of coloniser and colonised. This metaphorical exploration is embodied by the Candide-like Melog who sees, finds and even creates wonder everywhere he goes.

Apart from his own eccentric appearance and behaviour, Melog's Wales is fairly everyday, albeit mainly populated by roughnecks, a predominately sub-proletarian world of people on the dole with a 1970s flavour. This is either Morgan's jaundiced view of his country (or the valley towns where *Melog* is set) or satirical as in the clever chapter 'Public Executions' which explores rather well the role of bad news from the Third World in the more blessed lands of the West: 'You're looking at the familiar from a different angle, that's all. . . Some of us have to look at everything, even our own homeland, from a different position to everybody else' — which is in fact what this book attempts to do.

The land of 'Laxaria' where Melog supposedly comes from is a poignant, extreme version of Wales (or Catalonia or West Papua or. . .) where the native language has been outlawed and is preserved by just a few hundred nostalgic scholars and activists. At first bathetic, the plight of this imaginary people grows on the reader. The sadness of language decline and death is, after all, very real even if Morgan's 'Laxaria' isn't. There is something too of *Gulliver's Travels* here, with its strange lands so reminiscent of familiar ones all bathed in the mocking gleam of irony. There are also various symbolic characters and events, a patently mad old fellow ('Mr Job') copying out the classics of Welsh literature in longhand sending up no doubt impractical autodidactic schemes for the preservation of Welsh, and alluding to the shadow of cultural disaster that threatened the Welsh language through the twentieth century.

Serious themes treated lightly apart, there are lots of little pleasures here, including a loving description of low-rent or Bohemian domesticity. Melog's eternal bedsits are littered with crowds of 'cats like little lions' and the 'potato tavern' (i.e. chip shop) is the locus of much valleys social intercourse.

As the *Observer* put it, 'Originally published in Welsh, this extraordinary book shames us into realising that the best writers in Britain don't necessarily work in English'. This might also serve as motto for the Welsh-language section of this *Babel Guide*. RK

)) From the outside, the house of Ambrose Bing was an attempt to imitate number ten Downing Street in plastic, while inside it was luxurious without being tasteful. The floor was covered with a deep, orange shagpile carpet. In the middle of the carpet was an enormous red sofa. Sitting in the middle of this, bolt upright, his hands on his knees like a nervous child before the headmaster, as terrifyingly thin as ever and white as an apparition, was Melog. His skin was as if drawn taut across the nose and the sharpened cheek-bones. There were no cheeks, only grey hollows. The skull under the face was clearly visible. The blue eyes stared out of this background of deathly white. **((** 197

Prichard, Caradog

One Moonlit Night [Un Nos Ola Leuad]

One Moonlit Night doesn't have a clear-cut, linear narrative, as it is based on seemingly jumbled-up memories which pour haphazardly onto its pages. Yet a strong framework is provided by the moonlit night of the title, as the protagonist is a grown-up man who has returned to his native village after a period of incarceration for murder. As he walks around the village one night various places evoke scenes from his childhood and adolescence, and gradually his story builds up. An aura of mysteriousness surrounds him: he is unnamed, fatherless, and obsessed with his mad mother who spent the last part of her life in an asylum. The main character himself seems deranged (and the title is suggestive of lunacy), so that we seem to be looking into a cracked mirror where the image is all awry.

Although the story is narrated by one character, the perspective changes from time to time, which is both unsettling and exciting. At times the style is an adolescent's stream-of-consciousness, at others the voice of an adult narrator and yet again there are highly-charged, psalm-like, liturgical passages which convey his fantasy-driven imagination accented with madness.

Everything builds towards the climax where the protagonist walks away from the village towards the Dark Lake. It was here that he had his first sexual encounter around the age of sixteen, and strangled a young woman in a frenzy. The eroticism is not explicit, but suggested, which makes it all the more powerful. The same subtlety is used in implying the pull of the blue lake on the man's psyche, a magnetism which he seemingly cannot resist, and as he plunges into the depth of the water he is as if returning to his mother's womb.

One Moonlit Night is multi-layered, not only from the point of view of the shifting perspectives, but also in the way it portrays, not just one individual's complex psychology, but the nature of a whole society. That community lives in a slate-quarrying area in north Wales which suffered great deprivation around the beginning of the twentieth century, when there was a long strike lasting more than three years at the Penrhyn quarry, bringing humiliation to the quarrymen and their families. The book is undoubtedly partly autobiographical, as Caradog Prichard himself was brought up in a poor home in the quarry district by a mentally unstable mother, and he never knew his father as he had been killed in the quarry before he was born.

Although the pervading mood is gloomy, there are glimmers of humour. The innocence of childhood is invoked with great sensitivity, and much comedy springs from looking through a boy's eyes at events which he does not fully understand. A football match is described with great verve, and the visit of the circus provides a joyful distraction. One is also made aware of the influence of the Nonconformist religious revival which swept Wales early in the twentieth century. It isn't the theological aspects of this revival which are discussed, but the emotional, irrational effects, and the visit of a south Wales choir which sings a Welsh hymn with passion is described in very moving terms.

This is not a strictly realist novel, and has been described as 'proto-post-modernist'. Multifarious characters tumble across the pages as if out of a Hieronymus Bosch painting with plenty of sexual deviation, madness and anguish mixed with the comic elements. Nevertheless there is nothing obscure or difficult about the writing and it creates a fascinating social portrait.

The book can be described as Caradog Prichard's self-catharsis. He had been brought up in an almost monoglot Welsh community, and was not allowed the luxury of a higher education, yet he became a journalist, and spent most of his life in London's Fleet Street, culminating in work on the *Daily Telegraph*. He felt torn between his humble Welsh beginnings and his London existence. His literary soul was still in the Welsh-speaking Bethesda of his youth, and although earning his living through the medium of English in London, the language of his youth yet coursed through him so that his novel is the outpouring of an anguished exile, bringing to mind James Joyce's obsession with Dublin while living in Paris and Trieste. JR

)) And then I started crying. Not crying like I used to years ago whenever I fell down and hurt myself. . .

But crying like being sick.

Crying without caring who was looking at me.

Crying as though it was the end of the world.

Crying and screaming the place down, not caring who was listening.

And glad to be crying, the same way some people are glad when they're singing, and others are glad when they're laughing.

Dew*, I'd never cried like that before, and I've never cried like that since, either. I'd love to be able to cry like that again, just once more.

And I was still screaming and crying as I went out through the door and down the stone steps and along the gravel drive and through the gate onto the road, until I sat down by the side of the road by the gate. Then I stopped crying and started groaning, just like a cow groans when she's having a calf, then I started screaming and crying again. **((** 165

*Dew: Anglicised form of 'Duw', Welsh for God

Roberts, Kate

The Awakening [Y Byw sy'n Cysgu]

A woman's world within the man's world of the little quarry town of Aberentryd just after World War Two. We become witnesses to the exploding boil of a marriage break-up with its repercussions for all those involved.

Kate Roberts delivers us an X-ray plate of a household in a close-packed terrace, part of a small-scale, personalistic and familial world of So-and-So the teacher and Jones the lawyer. Although written from within the female character's point of view, even resorting to diary pages to give us ('the abandoned woman') Lora Ffenig's inner voice, somehow the male characters are more enjoyable. There's Uncle Edward 'wearing the same clothes he'd worn at the beginning of the century', whose mockable retro country manners and opinions warn of a fundamental division between town and country, or Lora Ffenig's brother-in-law Owen, whose tolerance and open-mindedness contrasts with the personalities of a group of rather rigid and dissatisfied female folk, and even Iolo the strayer who, one senses, will not find long-term joy with attractive husband-thief Mrs Amroth, 'as hard as Spanish iron'.

Lora's interactions with her children are charmingly, tenderly described: 'Come now, Mam's got a piece of chocolate for you after your milk'. As the book progresses all the neighbours and relatives — who immediately know Lora Ffenig's business — have a good old pick at the skeleton of her modest married happiness until eventually she discovers hubby was not merely a wanderer but a major all-round schlemiel.

However we judge wandering Iolo's misbehaviour, there is throughout the book, first published in Welsh in 1956, a (usually) gentle interrogation of the whole moralistic burden of chapel-Protestant Wales, described just before those particular walls of Jericho were about to tumble, from, amongst other factors, the impact of the war and the restlessness and dislocation it brought to formerly homogenous communities.

But Kate Roberts' *The Awakening*, albeit carrying a certain socio-cultural agenda of battles over 'respectability' long ago fought and won, is also a strangely moving account of people living — even if aware of the sacrifices it entailed — in an intimately known, familiar environment, a 'rooted community', something modern Britain has both largely escaped and yet widely regrets. Roberts transmits very warmly the small but important bliss of familiar places, of the stones, trees and hills that recognise us.

The Awakening is closely focused on women's lives in a particular place and time and yet not feminist. There is a certain coolness towards the female protagonists (who include housewives, teachers and secretaries) whilst the novel's ultimate emotional emphasis is, as revealed through the eyes of Lora's unsuccessful suitor, the dry lawyer, Aleth Meurig, on Lora's incarnation as mother-homemaker, the hearth goddess as cornerstone of happiness in life.

A peculiarity of the book is the wooden formality of the main character's speech, which has a distancing effect. Is the formality there to illustrate the character of Lora Ffenig, described by an unsuccessful suitor as 'warm, cold and distant at the same time'. Or is it a failure of style on Roberts' part faithfully carried over by the translator? Only a Welsh-speaker could possibly judge. RK

❱❱ They were all country people, and Welsh at that, and Welsh people couldn't usually enjoy pleasure because they were religious, and couldn't enjoy religion because they longed to pursue their appetites. 93

They were laughing over a story that Mr. Meurig told them about an old man from the country who'd come to make his will, and instead of naming the people who were to have his money, he'd named everyone who was to have nothing. 'This one — nothing. That one — nothing'. It was worth paying, the old man said, to show those devils how near they'd been to getting money from him. 84

Aleth Meurig went back to his home, put the electric fire on in his front parlour and sat in an easy chair. Staring into the fire and hardly knowing what he was doing, he slowly took a cigarette out of the packet. He'd gone across the road that evening full of hope that Lora would accept him. For some weeks now, she had filled his mind… he had recognised the meaning of true contentment as he'd sat at the tea table with her and the two children. There was something about her that radiated comfort. If he shut his eyes he could imagine he was with his mother. Motherly, that was the word. He began to question himself about the attraction of her house. Was it she herself, her beauty, or was it she herself in her home. There was wisdom in everything she'd said tonight. It seemed as though her unconscious mind was speaking from the past because she'd known how time could betray. **((** 196

Roberts, Kate

Feet in Chains [Traed Mewn Cyffion]

Feet in Chains by Kate Roberts is one of the most enduring Welsh-language novels of the twentieth century. In it, as in the entirety of her work, the author succeeds in capturing and committing to print the memory of a society destined to pass. Set in Roberts' native Arfon, which was a practically monolingual Welsh-speaking community until after World War Two, *Feet in Chains* records some forty years of the daily struggle with penury of a young couple, Ifan and Jane Gruffydd. Theirs' is the fight to rear a family on a modest quarry wage supplemented by subsistence farming. As with the other men-folk of the vicinity, Ifan's days are punctuated by the ringing of the quarry bell, while wife Jane labours season in season out to bring light and joy to the homestead.

Education provides the key for the next generation to escape a lifetime's hard toil. Blessed with the requisite intelligence, the Gruffydds' eldest son Owain takes a step towards emancipation when, due largely to his mother's encouragement, he wins a scholarship to the county school. If he accepts and attends, a career in teaching should be within his grasp. But the road to education is a long one, and the investment in time is one whose fruits the family may enjoy only in the seemingly distant future. Meantime, Ifan Gruffydd, no longer the young man he once was, feels the weight of years of work, and yearns for an apprentice's wage from the quarry to lighten his own load.

The path Owain will choose, whether gown or chisel, is fortuitous when compared to the ways of his sister, Sioned. Her weakness for fashion and urban delicacies, and her ineptitude as a breadwinner, soon come to cost the family dearly. Sioned begins to live away from home the better to practise her trade as a seamstress, but the move opens a gulf between daughter and parents. Her marriage to a local dandy completes the alienation, but when he abandons her for another, she is not ashamed to look to home for help to raise her little daughter.

In *Feet in Chains* we see one generation age as another matures, each confronting injustice and wrestling to rid themselves of the fetters which bind them to their station in life. But young and old, brother and sister are also bound together, and, though none is master of his destiny, a common will to endure and to overcome strengthens both family and community.

Kate Roberts' book features passages of prose justly held in high regard. The opening paragraphs well capture the mood of an outdoor sermon, the womenfolk's formal dress described in vivid detail and the preacher's voice droning on as young Jane Gruffydd feels faint in the heat. Other passages too are noteworthy. The death of Ifan Gruffydd's mother brings the question of will and property into focus. The old woman bequeaths all to her darling granddaughter, the deceitful Sioned. Outcry ensues among the older family members. Mustering all his resources, Ifan Gruffydd finds the words to resolve the dispute and keep the peace.

Feet in Chains tells of war years when Wales fed the battlefields of France with willing young men. Few families were spared grief and the Gruffydds are no exception. Were it not for the outbreak of hostilities, and the call to arms to protect smaller nations, Jane and Ifan's perseverance and dignity might have brought them some peace in their twilight years. But it's not to be: Owain's brother Twm,is killed in the trenches. The official telegram bearing the news from Her Majesty's forces is written in English, a language of which Jane Gruffydd knows not a word. Closing her eyes on this cruellest of days, she consoles herself with the thought that no longer will she fear the sound of the postman's approaching step. DJ

)) The hum of insects, gorse crackling, the murmur of heat, and the velvet tones of the preacher endlessly flowing. Were it not in the open air, most of the congregation would have been asleep. It was a Sunday in June and the Methodists of Moel Arian were holding their preaching festival in the open because the chapel could not hold this many people. It was the year 1880. **((7**

Roberts, Kate

A Summer Day and Other Stories

Kate Roberts was one of a very few women writers in Welsh to achieve prominence in the rather oppressive atmosphere of mid-twentieth century Wales, and this volume clearly demonstrates why she was able to make that breakthrough. Although the stories here were originally published in Welsh-language periodicals from 1925 to 1937, it was 1946 before this volume of beautifully-crafted translations brought them to the notice of a wider audience in Wales and outside. These are not proto-feminist texts, but they are written out of specifically female experience and no male Welsh writer of the time understood or conveyed as Roberts does the hidden heroism and tragedy of working-class women's existence in the quarry districts of north-west Wales.

These women show no self-pity, only endurance. Hemmed in by circumstances and narrow gender roles, Roberts' characters manage to achieve small moments of pleasure through simple things — paying off part of a debt, or drinking a cup of tea. Their dignity and determination is illustrated by trivial but symbolic acts of resistance. Pointless or ineffective as such defiance may be, it allows each to assert some individuality, some degree of control over her life against the odds and grab a tiny triumph in defeat. Thus Ffebi, faced with the sale of the family's goods in order to pay off debts, refuses to give up her beloved flannel quilt, itself bought, in wild defiance of poverty, as an object of pure beauty in her lacklustre life, whilst Sara in 'Sisters' fights to ensure that her dying sister recovers the dignity of cleanliness that had been the cornerstone of her being. The struggle is not always sweetened by emotional support from the spouse, as the young wife in 'The Loss' finds, suddenly realising that her plan to bring herself and her husband closer has in fact widened the gulf between them.

Even when a man was the main protagonist, Roberts, concentrating on what she knew best, usually brought him into the female territory of the home, whereas male writers of this period often focused on their own experience of life in more public arenas. The masculine role of her characters has been tempered by old age or illness, so that they are suddenly excluded from the outside world and masculine activity of quarry or farm, sustained only by memories of lost youth and vigour. The harshness of life is again tempered by the tenderness in these cameos, especially in 'The Condemned', where husband and wife retrieve, just before death finally parts them, something of their former close communication, lost for years to the demands of the daily grind.

Experience may often be gender-specific in a society where men and women occupy separate spheres for most of their waking hours, but in their different ways all cope as best they can with the universal struggles and tragedies of life. The focus of Roberts' work may be narrow, but, as the English novelist Storm Jameson writes in her foreword, 'in most of the stories there is a sense of wide space' and her characters' lives are lived as intensely and heroically as those of other writers painting on a broader canvas. CL-M

❱❱ There Ffebi met the greatest temptation of all in this period of stringency, a trial that called for all her strength. Blankets and handsome quilts, and in the middle, a quilt that made you catch your breath; that brought every woman there to finger it and look longingly at it as she walked away. A quilt of thick white Welsh flannel, with wavy stripes, green and blue, yellow and red, the fringe heavy and showing the close woven texture. She wanted to buy it, and the more she thought of her poverty, the greater grew her desire.

'Isn't it lovely?' her friend said. Ffebi did not reply, but stood spellbound. She left her friend and went in search of her husband and told him she wanted to buy it at once, before anybody else bought it. He looked at her uneasily, unwilling, and yet saying nothing. In the old days when money was plentiful, this would have made her change her mind. But her craving, the wild desire of a woman doomed, rode over all her emotions. She got the money and bought the quilt, took it home and spread it over the bed, burying her face in it to feel its texture. She almost longed for the winter to come. **((** 'The Quilt' 52

Roberts, Kate

Sun and Storm and Other Stories

This little collection is mainly composed of rather engrossing stories about a young Welsh maid, Winni, the classic naïve country girl, written no doubt from Kate Roberts' own rural background. Although Christmas puts in an appearance these are not sentimental tales: Winni's violent drunken father — an exultantly bad character — actually mugs her on the street for drinking money.

Winni's life centres on her affectionate relationships with her little half-brother and with her friends. Roberts shows us a hard-working put-upon life brightened only by the few hours spent with people she loves and by nature's beauty.

In 'Starting to Live' we meet a young married woman, Deina Prys, in her first weeks in her new cottage with her husband, a quarryman like the author's own people.

'Emptiness' is a story of Kate Roberts' old age about old age.

These six short pieces are an absolute showcase for Roberts' ineluctable narrative drive. However unattached one might feel to the inner life of a nineteenth-century Welsh maid or an old lady in hospital, the brio and staccato of Kate Roberts' prose draws you in. RK

)) There was a kind of devilish animal look about him at that minute, so that his daughter would have liked to strangle him. And crush his flesh until he was squashed like bad potatoes boiled for the pigs. 38

A December morning in a basement in the town; the gas light hissing like a snake all the time; the sound of people walking on the pavement outside and banging the grating like a child striking one note on the piano all day, and Winni trying to please her mistress by cleaning the flues of the big old double-ovened stove. It would be easier to do this if Robert, the four year old child were to stay with his mother on the floor above. But he would insist on being with Winni, and by now there was the same amount of soot on both their faces. **((** 'Oh! Winni! Winni!' 28

Roberts, Kate

Tea in the Heather [Te yn y Grug]

Set against the backdrop of the slate-quarrying heartland of Gwynedd at the turn of the twentieth century, *Tea in the Heather* is Wyn Griffith's accomplished translation of *Te yn y Grug*, one of Kate Roberts' finest achievements. First published in 1959, it is a masterful work that can be considered as both novel and short-story collection, with an episodic structure charting the development of young Begw Gruffudd between the ages of four and nine years old. Begw is a young child coming to terms with the harsh realities of rural life in the Wales of her time and her brief confrontations with death, disappointment, loss and estrangement mark the beginnings of her adulthood with the gradual realisation 'she herself would have to stand on her own two feet one day': a rather frightening premise for a young child.

Despite being the depiction of a child's world, this is a peculiarly sophisticated and multi-layered text, in which the elaboration of single, seemingly inconsequential events are fused with understated complexity and canny character judgement. *Tea in the Heather* is an astute exploration of a child's consciousness in a world of adult values, and as it begins the four-year-old Begw is seen to be experiencing sorrow for the first time, contemplating the dead body of her drowned cat, Sgiatan. The details are rendered with wondrous simplicity: 'In all four years of her life, this was the most distressing day Begw had known, a black hopeless day, although the world was white with snow'. And in the cyclical trend of such narratives, it is at this cold place that Begw finds herself again at the end of the novel, when 'a feeling of dread came over her' in realising that there are limitations to her childhood world, as she edges nearer to the brink of adulthood.

However *Tea in the Heather* is not as dark as it may first appear, for the child's world is also seen to be a colourful, idealistic place, often depicted with wry humour. Through the use of particularly buoyant and rhythmic dialogue, the people in Begw's world come to us vividly and her characteristically strong female protagonists tower comically above meagre male counterparts. It is during this collection that we are first introduced to one of Roberts' finest character creations, the wild Winni Ffinni Hadog, the unconstrained, intrepid, and yet vulnerable older girl who presents to Begw an exciting, dark, limitless alternative to her own simple, one-dimensional world. Winni represents to the reader not only the mysterious side of humanity, but also marks an otherness in Roberts' writing, an eccentricity at the core of her apparently conservative literary temperament.

Roberts's descriptive prowess enables *Tea in the Heather* to become a universal exploration of the concerns of family and community, while also providing a particular vibrant slice-of-life of the Welsh-language communities of this era. It is also inexorably bound to a key theme of Kate Roberts: disappointment. And while this may not seem the most exhilarating of themes, it is executed in such a way that it enables the reader to take comfort in the simple pleasures of life, such as the freedom to roam the countryside, to discover new words and envisage other worlds, and to take control of one's own life. Despite our daily disappointments, Roberts reminds us that there is always the concept of 'tea in the heather', and the frivolity, wonder, and freedom this represents. FfD

)) Begw ran on and on, feeling as light as air, until she reached an iron stile, over it, and on to a wide flat moor, running on until she found herself going downhill and in sight of a valley with a river. She stopped and sat down on a soft tuft of moss, still sobbing, with now and then a cry of shame at her disgrace, miserable because no one except her mother had ever whipped her. Then another thought crossed her mind, that she had just begun to see something she liked in Winni, instead of being like everyone else in the village, looking upon her as a heap of dung you wouldn't touch with a pitchfork. **((** 46.

Roberts, Kate

Two Old Men and Other Stories

This special illustrated edition of a handful of Kate Roberts' stories was produced in honour of her ninetieth birthday. Kyffin Williams' fourteen or so accompanying linocuts can be described as both warm and slate-like in their solidity and flatness. There is also a short laudatory introduction by John Gwilym Jones that breathes those most revered names of classic shortstorydom, Maupassant and Chekhov. He also reminds us of Roberts' 'intuitive recognition of human relationships'. Perhaps Kate Roberts is not quite as subtle and witty as The Big M or Even Bigger C but she sat closer to the ordinary mortal. Her stories are as soft, warm and delicately healing as Williams' best images.

The title piece 'Two Old Men' seems simple and straightforward at first — but is it a morality tale, an *aperçu* of a writer's life, or a vision of ageing and loneliness?

Reading Kate Roberts today invites us to recall a more effortful but perhaps cosier form of domesticity before television and the rest of passive 'all-electric living' took over our evenings: 'He poked the fire and moved the kettle onto it; in no time at all there was a good fire and a singing kettle'.

The story entitled 'The Treasure', although about a satisfying and prodigal friendship between two older women, is still a bleak tale — with the Maupassantian chill of summoning reality rather than the women's magazine cop-out glow — the nub of it is the regretted absence of achieved and lasting love in both their lives.

'Visiting', however, is short and blazing, and here Kate Roberts surely shows us some of Chekhov's glow, the ability to capture a huge chunk of feeling in a few flat writerly strokes, in a few dozen paragraphs.

The last story, 'Winter Fair', catches the end of the seasonal fairs and their enormous significance for country people, to trade livestock, hire hands and maids, to generally enjoy themselves and to meet up with everyone in their social world — a glorious experience for folk who barely travelled or indeed rested from their labours of husbandry, housekeeping and arable farming. RK

)) . . . she went into Marshalls and sat down to wait for Ben. She enjoyed being there enormously. Carpets to walk on, nice food and flowers, plenty of people; the food was so different from her usual fare.

Her pastrycrust was never a success. It was like old shoe leather.

And how could it be otherwise with a broken oven? And no hope of having it mended so long as her mother-in-law insisted that it was fine; that it had baked well enough for her for the last twenty years. Perhaps it did bake bread; but why should one bake bread when the van called daily? But as for a pastrycrust, you could not buy it in the country. Today, at any rate, she would have tiny pink and yellow cakes, and pastry which looked as if it had been blown up, with cream inside. Oh, she was so happy — except when she remembered her mother-in-law. That was the only fly in the ointment. Her words before they left today echoed in her ears. 'I don't know why you have to go to Fair with things as they are. And for that matter, there is no Winter Fair now as there was in the old days. There is no home-made cheese, no wigs, no griddle-cakes, nothing of the sort and nobody like the old Bardd Crwst, to sing his ballads'.

To tell the plain truth, her mother-in-law was a nuisance with her 'old days' over and over again, carrying on about the wastefulness of the present age. What if she knew that her daughter-in-law had face-powder in her bag now? And what if she knew that Ben would pay four shillings for tea for two? Presently, Ben arrived in a surge of people that made the room look almost full. The whole atmosphere exuded warmth and the electric light shone brightly on the aluminium teapots.

Ben had not enjoyed himself all that much at the football ground. The old fierce spirit which had burnt once so brightly between Town and Holyhead had died.

The two enjoyed their tea. **((** 'Winter Fair' 77

Roberts, Kate

The World of Kate Roberts: Selected Stories 1925–1981

This is a definitive collection of Kate Roberts' stories compiled shortly after her death in 1985. Rather than being the work of a major British publisher, proud to have this flag-bearer and innovator of Welsh literature on their list, it comes from Temple University Press in New Jersey who have a strong international and translated literature list. Copies both new and used are easy enough to find on the Internet but library copies are infrequent in the UK. This is an essential book for anyone with a real interest in Welsh-language fiction because here one can see the breadth and development of this important and genial author.

Her translator, Joseph P. Clancy, notes in his introduction that Kate Roberts is exercised by cultural and spiritual impoverishment as well as the economic kind. This makes her almost uncannily relevant in this period of dumbing down and global-disposable culture.

The volume starts with autobiographical excerpts, lamenting the impoverishment of the Welsh spoken in Denbigh where she made her home and telling us too how much her writing is drawn from personal experience: 'they (her family — Ed.) wove my destiny in the distant past'. Here we can sense the connectedness of a writer embedded in a definable community, something that in twentieth century literature has coexisted with the more frankly cosmopolitan and alienated type of writer from Kafka through Bellow to Atwood. The blank, hard and truthful style of her autobiographical writing, however, is not at all cosy and can be quite devastating.

From the early stories of 1925–37, 'The Letter' is brief and powerful, and describes with humour an episode from the life of the educationally disenfranchised. 'The Loss' is a despatch from the matrimonial front, where Roberts became something of a war correspondent, here reporting the cold death of romance and romantic expectations confronted with everyday life. In these stories we have Roberts' early exhibition pieces with her trademark homely details, which somehow escape banality, the bacon frying and boiled egg with tea and 'thin bread and butter'. 'Protest March' is quite a complex tale about marriage, poverty and politics from the perspective of a couple living in an underground kitchen.

From 1949 comes 'Gossip Row', a novella in diary form and an attempt at a woman's narrative which suffers from an unconvincing voice.

The short stories of *Tea in the Heather* signalled (in 1959) Roberts' return to that form but with a greater than ever economy of style. In 'Grief' there is the little girl who after the death of her cat has cried so much onto her wooden doll that the paint runs. The story speaks to the untutored feminine emotionality at the root of much of this author's work.

These stories, centred on young Begw, are potent in their ability to give voice to a child's feelings and worldview. They are a startling embodiment of a child's life and thoughts from early twentieth-century rural Wales. Begw has a snobbish friend (with whom she endlessly competes) from next door and there is jealousy of her brother's rough-and-tumbling on the nutting and blackberrying expeditions for which a young girl is considered too delicate.

'Dark Tonight' is a novella from 1962, based around a middle-aged Minister's wife and her social circle, that has, as ever, lovely minor domestic detail: 'Nel the cat runs into the back kitchen with her tail up to get a saucer of milk'.

The final section of the book is 'Stories 1964–1981', from the last part of this long literary career. Here are included stories of old people as in 'Flowers' where old Gwen Huws recalls the folk of her little town. 'The Journey' is a poignant story of a young man leaving Arfon (Roberts' own home region in north Wales) to work in south Wales: 'He couldn't forget Alis' face last night as she said goodbye; her eyes were bright with hope, longing fearlessly to be able to come to him in the South and settle there. In thinking of this his heart became a block of ice; he wasn't going to the South to settle, but going there thinking he could return'.

Another less obvious side to Kate Roberts' work is her humour, as in the 'Battle of Christmas' about a toyshop keeper, which invokes the struggle of Mrs Jones next-door with Mrs Jones next-door-down, accompanied by the obnoxious Polly Parrot screaming the place down, but this is also a sweet and homely story of inclusive and kindly Christmas spirit.

In a very different but equally humane mood 'Hope' goes deep, fascinatingly deep into the mother–child bond. This should be required reading for all new fathers.

'Return' is haunting, the usual domestic simplicities, dough cakes and pussy cats and plain Welsh folk but set in a cascading chain of times and realities to create a hyper-reality in the writing itself. This is one of Kate Roberts' best and most technically advanced pieces.

'Tomorrow and Tomorrow' tracks the part-confused, part-acute thought processes of an old lady and is also a virtuoso piece.

A heavyweight book of heartfelt work. RK

)) The walk from Llanwerful, the place where the bus stopped, up to the lake was hot, and it was good to sit on its bank in spite of the insects that were whirling around their noses. After they came within sight of the lake Annie saw two things to worry her. Three motor cars at the lakeside was the first thing—high and mighty people's cars.

'Why couldn't these people leave their cars at Llanwerful, instead of bringing them to the lakeside?' she said.

'Yes,' he said, 'it would do double-chinned people like this good to walk, and it would be good for the scenery to be without them and their cars.' 'The Loss' 53

As usual, too, Gruff's friends came, two ministers and one priest. That was the high point of our holidays. We were a close-knit group around the tea table in the cottage, Geraint and his friend Gwilym who was camping with him in the field having gone out in the boat. I could create an illusion about the four men and put them in one of the restaurants I'd read about in the big cities. They were arguing like those literary men and their clothes were just as untidy. No one would have thought they were any different from the debaters in city restaurants. Wil was the thunderer, When he came through the door he was like a heavy-laden ship and the top of his head almost struck the crossbeam, his hat turned up in front, a scarf around his neck, wearing a raincoat, its pockets bulging out like a mule's packs with books, and high boots on his feet. Before asking how anyone was,

'What do you think of this, Gruff?' producing the Steddfod compositions from one of his pockets.

'I enjoyed it very much'.

'Enjoyed, enjoyed,' Wil shouted, 'enjoyed such rubbish. A man looks forward each year to seeing a particle of genius, and there's not a thing there but a bit of talent with some varnish on it'.

'What do you hope to find?' Jac the parson asked.

'A little trace of vision. Here we are, living in the most turbulent age the world's ever seen, and these poets don't see anything in it but a chance to describe, describe the horrors of war, describe the effect of the new age on the Welsh way of life, the world changing, nostalgia for the old things and continually lamenting over the loss. There isn't one of them has the guts to open his own soul and see what's there'.

'You're right,' Jac said, 'we've become too peaceable or too torpid. A man needs to battle before he can write. Something has to stir him up'. **((** 'Dark Tonight' 243

Roberts, Wiliam Owen

Pestilence [Y Pla]

Wiliam Owen Roberts' *Pestilence* is a work whose vision and depth has rarely been equalled in modern Welsh writing. A historical novel set in the mid-fourteenth century, it is a study in the instigation of change, the forces which cause change, and ways in which people and society react and adapt to change. The context for this study is, on the one hand, feudal Wales, and, on the other, a Europe prey to the Black Death, ruled by insouciant monarchs, and animated by apocalyptic religious zeal.

The reader is invited to explore the lives of Welsh serf and lord, sheriff, soldier and clergyman in the time after Edward II's conquest of the country, and the demise of the indigenous Welsh princes and their authority.

The context is of disenfranchisement and a political interregnum in the last decades of medieval isolation in what *Pestilence* portays as a moribund system. It is a tired society with violence ever present, and no-one imagines a change in their lot other than an increase or decrease in suffering and abjectness.

The dogmas of a highly institutionalised and hierarchical Roman Catholic Church define the world of Chwilen Bwm, the leper whose primary pleasure is derived from sexually abusing his goat. Sharing a fief with serf and leper we find Lady Angharad whose frustrations and superstitions make of her a pale non-persona. Divorced from the harsh but ordered cycle of seasonal labour in the fields, Lady Angharad, noble, female and idle, inches ever closer to insanity as, unknown to all, the Black Death approaches.

The book follows the devastating spread of the plague from the point of its initial outbreak in the Levant through the ports of the Mediterranean, Adriatic and Tyrrhenian seas and then into Western Europe.

Travelling on a trading vessel from Cairo, Salah Ibn al Khatib, student of the Koran and son of an Egyptian notary, has been charged by his father with a mission none other than to make his way to Paris and there to bring about the death of the King of France.

Salah sets out, innocent to the ways of the world, but emboldened by his promise to his father. When his ship is refused access to an Italian port, the bewildered, disorientated young Muslim finds himself crossing first Italy, then France in the company of a cortege of monks. On the way, he encounters social turmoil and religious zeal, abandoned and wasted villages and homesteads, things Wiliam Owen Roberts writes of as Chaucer or Boccacio did while depicting, Brueghel-like, the grotesque side of a society on the brink of anarchy.

The better to make good time on his way to Paris and fulfil his mission Salah Ibn al Khatib bargains with a rustic giant for an old nag in the city of Florence. Soon, however, he finds himself lying naked in the nocturnal mud, his money pocketed by a cunning seductress and his destiny growing ever darker by the hour.

The book weaves these and other strands into a gripping narrative which witnesses the old status quo in Wales collapse leaving a vacuum to be filled by a new social order. As such, *Pestilence* is a study of the effects of global phenomena on local circumstances, in this instance, things whose origins, though distant, send their shockwaves right through to Eifionydd in north Wales.

Pestilence established Wiliam Owen Roberts as a significant novelist on both the national and international stages. In it, he developed a rich, idiosyncratic idiom to transport a complex plot while giving voice to the fears and hopes of a large cast of memorable characters. DJ

)) On Palm Sunday the serfs threw flowers on the graves as a symbol of the Resurrection. Iorwerth Gam was buried in Holy Week.

Chwilen Bwm wasn't feeling at all well. The heavy cold he had seemed to be spreading throughout his body and his bones ached. All night long he tossed on his straw.

The coffin, the coffin. . .

They all came out of the church and walked towards the graveyard, carrying candles, and singing as they went.

Succour his soul, ye saints of God. Bear him to light eternal, ye angels and archangels. . .

The coffin was lowered slowly into the earth, Iorwerth Gam of the tenantlands descending into the dark soil.

Weeping, weeping. . .

Through it all, he was aware of Nest, daughter of Iorwerth Gam, aware of her face, her eyes, her hands, her thin ankles. He crept close to her as she stood at the graveside, and snuffled, snorted, sniffed at her. In spite of his cold, he could smell her, and the Easter earth, and the sweat of freemen and serfs, but above all the smell of Nest, daughter of Iorwerth Gam, as she kissed the mounded earth. **((** 136–7

Rowlands, John

A Taste of Apples [Ienctid yw 'Mhechod]

The scandal of a passionate affair between a married minister of religion and an attractive young woman from his congregation is still a favourite with newspapers, but in chapel-going Wales in 1965 it was nothing short of dynamite. In this short novel Emrys, trapped in his loveless marriage with the frigid Gwen, becomes sexually obsessed with Elsa, to the extent that he begins to question his faith and the purpose of his ministry. At the same time he manages to convince himself that what he feels for her is not simply lust but real love and that he somehow has God's approval for his behaviour. Pastoral visits to Elsa's bedridden mother provide opportunities for the lovers, demonstrating how far his relationship with her has taken him from the straight and narrow: the scene where they make love on the parlour floor while Elsa's mother lies dying upstairs retains its power to shock even today. The old woman's death that night brings Elsa to a sharp realisation of her situation and, poignantly, of the wrong she is doing to Emrys' wife. Through Elsa's brave efforts, she and Gwen become reconciled whilst Emrys collapses into a breakdown.

With hindsight, we can see that traditional Welsh society was at a crossroads when the novel first came out. As the 1960s progressed, economic and social changes and increasing English influence went hand-in-hand with the beginnings of secularisation. The stranglehold of chapel began to slacken as post-war baby-boomers preferred dancing to the sounds of the Swinging Sixties to singing hymns and attending Sunday School. Published at a moment when life in Welsh-speaking communities was in a state of flux, this novel, shining a bright light on a pastor's 'feet of clay', was extraordinarily brave. Not only that, *A Taste of Apples* was also ahead of its time in its sensitive treatment of the classic love triangle, accepting that individuals can be at the mercy of their passions whilst not neglecting to remind us that our behaviour affects, often hurts, others close to us. But Emrys is too obsessed with his lover to care that his position as minister to his flock brings responsibilities to the wider community too, and that these are inevitably compromised by his affair, as much when it is over as during it. It is Elsa, the 'scarlet woman', who emerges as the most honest and responsible of all three protagonists.

The book could be described as one of Wales' early feminist novels, not least for its happy acceptance of strong but not predatory female sexuality, and what must have been one of the first explicit celebrations of female orgasm in modern Welsh literature. Although the story is told mainly from the minister's point of view, Elsa and Gwen's complex feelings and reactions to events are analysed as carefully as his; both women emerge from the unhappy affair stronger and with greater self-understanding, their increasing confidence paralleled in Emrys' downward slide. Perhaps it was not just the sex but its honesty and humanity in depicting these events which made *A Taste of Apples* seem so shocking to its first readers and makes it still worth reading today. CL-M

)) It was pleasant to lay her hand again on the electric kettle and feel its warmth, and to enjoy cutting bread and butter. Gwen came to lend a hand. Though so utterly different the two women had drawn very close together. In some mysterious way they understood each other's weaknesses and acknowledged the difference between them. Were Emrys to come in then how would they react to him? He would seem to be a complete stranger and they would try to defend each other from him. Yet Emrys' body had known both their bodies. Elsa again felt the urge to hold Gwen closely to her but knew instinctively that the other would shrink back into her shell and would not relish close contact of that kind. She could not imagine Gwen giving herself to any man — to anyone at all, for that matter. Probably she was happier for that reason and was keeping herself clean and safe in the glass cupboard of her life. Nevertheless she had given something of herself to Elsa this afternoon. When she had burst into tears Gwen had come to console her. So, after all, it was possible to soften the stone. **((** 60

Thomas, R.S.

Autobiographies [Neb]

[This autobiographical work does not fit precisely the *Babel Guide* scheme but is included for the importance of the writer. RK]

Asked to name two great Welsh poets of the twentieth century many people would mention Dylan Thomas and R.S. Thomas. As it happens both were born within a year of one another: Dylan in 1914 in Swansea and Ronald Stewart in 1913 in Cardiff. When Dylan Thomas died notoriously in Manhattan of an 'insult to the brain' in 1953, this was still three years before R.S. published his acclaimed first major collection, *Song at the Year's Turning* (1955). It was John Betjeman, in a generous introduction to this work, who said that R.S. Thomas' poetry would outlive his own. Whether or not Betjeman is yet the forgotten muse, it is safe to say that R.S. Thomas' productivity and longevity (he finally died aged 87 in 2000) mean that his legacy eclipses that of the other Thomas, not least taking into account his 1996 Nobel Prize for literature nomination. Over 1,500 poems are available, all inflected by the same spare lyricism invoking the spirit and nature of Welsh peasant folkways and the wildlife and geology of the land, a testament to the spiritual quest of a man who spent his life as an Anglican cleric ministering to small rural parishes. His life describes, as he wrote in his autobiographical fragment 'Neb', a sort of oval through the geography of Wales; from Holyhead, where he grew up, to the Llŷn peninsula, where he spent his last years of retirement and contemplation.

Both poets expressed themselves in English although for R.S. this is no choice but more like a wound (a metaphor much used by Arab authors of North Africa who write in French). While both men were given to expressing negative feelings for the Welsh people, it was R.S. who saw their salvation in the one cultural attribute that could single them out in the dreary modern world of machines (he was said by his son, Gwydion, to have preached sermons on the evils of refrigerators) and the dreaded English. That was their unique linguistic inheritance. Coming himself only late to the Welsh tongue (he took to it only in his thirties) he never felt sufficiently its master to compose poetry in it, limiting himself to hymns and the odd autobiographical piece. He took to Welsh, he writes in the essay 'Former Paths', in order to return to the 'true Wales' of his imagination. It is these Welsh autobiographical writings which are reviewed here. The collection comprises four pieces. The most substantial is 'Neb' which can be read as 'No-one', but, as translator Jason Walford Davies points out in his introduction, this rendition is by no means straightforward. In essence, the piece is a third-person account of the poet's life written in a spare, unemotional tone. He speaks of R.S'.s childhood, his experiences of education and his working life and its concomitant peregrinations. There is buried in the narrative an almost willed naïveté. He is not seeking to embellish the life or demonstrate his sophistication, for he is too humble a man for that. Faced with the wonders of creation, exemplified by nature and, above all, by the world of birds, simplicity of expression becomes the only legitimate form of honesty. It is the same tone that inhabits 'Former Paths' but the device of the third-person narrator is here dropped. In 'The Creative Writer's Suicide' he addresses his own predicament of coming late to the language, but realising its crucial importance for preserving a small nation and its traditions. The last piece in the collection, 'A Year in Llŷn', takes the form of a monthly diary, beautifully interweaving reflections on Wales and the threat posed by the encroachments of the English with acute observations of birds and the natural world and ruminations on poetry. These writings serve as a backdrop to the poetry but the life of the man cannot prepare us for the full range of his poetic work. They do help us, however, to escape the more tabloid press stereotypes of the rabid nationalist poet and cleric who allegedly advocated the torching of English-owned holiday homes in Wales.

Certainly, Thomas was contradictory and complex, as biographer Byron Rogers suggested in his insightful *The Man Who Went into the West* (2006), but we must also be able to let the poetry stand alone. GS

▶▶ Time was when these people used to come here in August and then go home. Some in Llŷn were glad to see them, and glad of the little money that came with them to help make ends meet. Now they are like a millstone about our necks all year round and have created more problems than they have solved. Personally I know how to avoid them. The fields and the hedgerows and the woods are still free of them. And if you are willing to weave through them on Mynydd Mawr you can still find a secluded spot in the rocks somewhere between the sea and sky. Or you can get up early and go out for an hour of quiet before the campers have stirred. All this in the knowledge that it will become worse in August, when the schools have closed. But however that may be, in August the migratory birds start their passage, and if there's a storm, it is worth going out, tourists or not, to see what is happening on the sea. August did I say? The waders start on their journey south in this month. As early as the second day, I have seen the green sandpiper on the edge of Ty Mawr pool, and no sooner does the last whimbrel pass by on its way north, than the first one of the autumn is on its way south. Nature never loiters. The birds crave mobility the same as the motorists, but less expensively, with a more melodious cry, and less dangerously. **((** 'A Year in Llŷn' 148

Williams, D.J.

The Old Farmhouse [Hen Dŷ Ffarm]

Here is a seemingly simple stream of reminiscences of rural life in north Carmarthen in the late nineteenth century: lyrical evocations of a lad's first six years on the family farm. The six-year-old's eyes record and recreate a world and a way of life but the adult narrator simultaneously re-enacts the loss of it. We become aware of the disjunction between an 'all one long today, dateless, endless and carefree' and 'the day we left Penrhiw [the family farm, Ed.] at the beginning of October 1891', made all the more poignant because the narrative's past, present and future is already lost for the twenty-first-century reader.

D.J. Williams' easy and intimate storyteller's style recreates what he sees as the lost values of belonging and community in a rural idyll overtaken by industrialisation's disconnection and dislocation. Rather than being a homily, *The Old Farmhouse* is a rooted, earthy celebration. The narrative is full of naming sequences, for places ('Llanedi and Capadochia and ffair y Bont'), people and beloved farm animals. 'It took possession of me,' he writes of his country, 'and I have taken possession of it...' In the naming, his dream of returning ('a dream now that will never come true') to an idyllic past is realised, and possesses the present for both author and reader in a powerful way.

To be a 'man of the Square Mile' (dyn y filltir sgwâr) — i.e. a local man in every sense — is a Welsh concept which epitomises this book's ideals, and *The Old Farmhouse* resounds with sense of place. 'When the many things I remember actually happened... I haven't much of an idea. But I can locate most of them with a degree of certainty,' claims the book's narrator. Like one of his characters, the skill lies in effortlessly 'making a continent so rich in interest of his own country,' the very absence of great events making room for the humorous anecdotes and wry observations which crowd the book and give insight into a whole rural community, peopled with extraordinary individuals — both human and animal.

By means of the self-effacing device of an autobiographical account through a child's eyes, we are drawn unsuspectingly into the absorbingly self-referential world of Rhydcymerau. Simultaneously, the character of John Jenkins — the larger-than-life drover, dealer and innkeeper — provides an alter ego for the adult storyteller. Both tell tales 'clearly and concisely' and with 'grand hyperbole'; both have 'the hidden energy of a precious historical instinct'.

The Old Farmhouse was the volume chosen by UNESCO to represent Welsh literature in its mid-twentieth-century series of translations from minority languages, and it was translated by the Welsh poet, Waldo Williams. However, another poet from north Carmarthenshire claimed that the volume gave too rosy an account of agricultural reality. In fact, despite the claims to veracity made by this genre of rural novel, this is a delightfully subjective account, hedged by real people and places on one side and a dreamlike quality on the other as the narrator relives the 'unspoiled rural life I have loved so much in reminiscences all my life...' It is also a haunting reading experience, whereby a visit to the other country of the narrator's past magically superimposes itself on the reader's own map of Wales. AB

)) But I was getting to this. Many times in Penrhiw I remember my elders speaking of a flock of pheasants or a covey of partridges in this field or that, someone counting them, perhaps, and another wondering whether he was correct and counting them for himself again after they had spread out or gathered closer as they busily gleaned the ears of corn left on the stubble — or perhaps the young cocks would be pretending to jump at each other for a moment or two before they returned to what they were at. I couldn't see them at all. Certainly I couldn't see them. And I knew that, too, somewhere down on the bottom of my mind, had I the patience or the honesty to go down there. But the talk and the descriptions by those who had good eyes were so lively and my interest in these beautiful birds was so great and my imagination was so much more alive than my conscience that I definitely believed — I don't in the world know how — I believed that I saw with my own eyes of flesh everything that went on: unknown to me my short sight had extended my imagination and made me an excellent and perfectly honest little fibber. And who can blame a good liar, after all, after getting to know all about him? **((** 238–240

Modern Welsh-language poetry in English translation

Poetry in the Welsh language can be traced to the beginning of the medieval period. In the European context, this depth of tradition can be matched only by Irish poetry. Both Welsh and Irish traditions predate by entire centuries literature in other European vernaculars. Unlike Irish, however, which underwent major change towards the end of the first millennium CE*, poetry written in Welsh since the earliest times can, with a little orthographical modification, be deciphered and partially understood by the educated modern reader. Thus, in Welsh, it is possible to speak of an unbroken tradition stretching back a millennium and a half.

Welsh is a language whose roots lie in the pre-Roman Celtic language of Britain called Brythonic. Welsh was to be the principal spoken language in Wales until the early twentieth century.

However, as the twentieth century progressed, Welsh was increasingly perceived by its custodians as being a language in crisis. This state of crisis is one of the themes explored by its modern poets. Gwyn Thomas writes: 'Those of us still left, aren't we like piranha in a bowl here, intent on devouring each other?' (**BBMWP, 256) The crisis of language is matched by the crisis facing community. Alun Cilie writes of The Old Chapel: 'Gone the flame, gone the bustle; and the pulpit now is mute' (BBMWP, 92).

Translation of modern Welsh poetry falls into two categories. One is academic. Various scholars of literature have, in recent decades, striven to translate the Welsh poetry of various centuries. The purpose of translation of this kind has been to raise awareness of the existence and riches of Welsh literature. The second category of translation — the translation of contemporary authors — is a recent phenomenon, with a more specific purpose. The publishing of the translation forms an important part of the poets' and their publishers' attempt to increase these poets' success and to market their work. This may be attributable in part to the fact that the pool of readers of Welsh poetry in Welsh is too small to sustain poetic careers. However, it brings into focus certain complex questions. For example, when or to what degree does translation contribute to the redundancy and irrelevance of the Welsh original? On the other hand, it is probable that increased interest in translation reflects increasing awareness of poetry in Welsh, this in turn creating synergy between authors and their public.

A word about certain forms of Welsh poetry is essential to an appreciation of the culture of translation. Two types are discernable. These are the native and the innovative. Native Welsh poetry is generally classical in form, this meaning that it has, during its history, subscribed to sophisticated systems of rhyme and metre. Innovation in the tradition has often meant adopting English forms, whether the sonnet or free verse, for example.

Translating native Welsh poetry, one is confronted with the questions how best to represent the sonorous and rhythmic qualities of the original, to what extent this is possible, and to what extent one must resign oneself to a simple echoing of the semantics of the original. It should be stressed that the classical native forms — *englyn, cywydd, awdl* written in *cynghanedd* metre — are thriving modern forms, just as they were in the fourteenth century.

The translation of modern Welsh poetry falls into two periods. The first dates from World War One until 1967. In that year Tony Conran published his *Welsh Verse* (reprinted by publishers Seren in 1992 and 2003). The second period runs from 1967 until the present day, a time during which Welsh poetry forms an ever-closer bond with its sister corpus of translations.

Among the eminent poets featured in Conran's *Welsh Verse* are T. H.Parry-Williams, Saunders Lewis, David Gwenallt Jones, Waldo Williams, Bobi Jones and Gwyn Thomas. These individuals, all male, carry between them the banner of Welsh poetry from about 1900 to 1967. All are poets who have bequeathed us a body of work, a style, and a philosophy. Parry-Williams' work is often an expression of the importance of place: 'The mountains' primitive forms pressed in till their barrenness penetrated my bone' (BBMWP, 68). Saunders Lewis often alluded to the idea of European civilisation of which Wales for him was part. In a long poem 'The Deluge 1939' he writes of 'dragon's teeth sown over Europe's acres'. David Gwenallt Jones comments on the consequences of industrial life in the south: 'Workers tramp shadowless from place to place' (BBMWP, 98). Waldo Williams is admired for principles of pacifism, while, as a learner of the language, Bobi Jones is concerned with the self as an expression of a culture. Gwyn Thomas, on the other hand, writes in a humanist vein: 'Congratulations. Well done. Twelve dead; two men burnt to black cinders; ten more persons mutilated' (BBMWP, 257).

Books published since 1967 which are central to a reading of Welsh poetry in translation are *The Poetry of Wales 1930–1970* (ed. R. Gerallt Jones, Gomer 1974); *Twentieth Century Welsh Poems* (Joseph P. Clancy, Gomer 1982); *Modern Poetry in Translation (Welsh Issue)* (ed. D. Johnston, University of London 1995); *The Peacemakers* by Waldo Williams (tr. T.Conran, Gomer 1997); *The Adulterer's Tongue*, (R. Minhinnick, Carcanet 2003); *Welsh Women's Poetry 1460–2001*, (eds. K. Gramich, C. Brennan, Honno 2003) *The Bloodaxe Book of Modern Welsh Poetry* (eds. M. Elfyn, J. Rowlands, Bloodaxe 2003).

Poets featured in *The Adulterer's Tongue* include Emyr Lewis, Iwan Llwyd, Gwyneth Lewis and Elin ap Hywel. Poets featured in *Modern Poetry in*

Translation, other than those already cited include Alan Llwyd, Gerallt Lloyd Owen and Elin Llwyd Morgan. These poets, viewed collectively, represent, in an international context, a post-war generation, and, in a national context, a generation during whose time Welsh speakers claimed and were granted certain civic rights. In this, their world differs vastly from poets born earlier. In other ways, the group is heterogeneous, but its composition also reflects an increased presence of women in the ranks of Welsh literati.

The *Bloodaxe Book of Modern Welsh Poetry* (eds. Elfyn, Rowlands), being a recent and comprehensive anthology, is worth alluding to in some detail. The anthology is panoramic and pioneering. It permits the English-speaking reader an appreciation of the depth and breadth of Welsh poetry in the twentieth century, and, as such, reflects aspects of the reality of the tradition as seen from within. Rather than focusing solely on major poets, the book also features major poems.

The host of names included here also reflects the fact that, during the twentieth century, while many people wrote in Welsh, most did so only on occasion, perhaps to enjoy participating in competitions such as the Eisteddfod, and that their poetic output may be represented by a small handful of well-crafted but not necessarily innovative texts.

Poems in the *Bloodaxe Book* which the reader might particularly enjoy are: Pwllderi, Dewi Emrys (48); Rebirth, Mererid Hopwood (402); Goddesses, Elin ap Hywel (384); The Language Murderer, Gwyneth Lewis (364); The Moons of Llŷn, Alan Llwyd (302). The reader is also encouraged to seek out the following poems in other collections: Cilmeri (Gerallt Lloyd Owen, in *Modern Poetry in Translation* (Welsh Issue), 126); Y Tangnefeddwyr, in *Welsh Verse*, 90), and The Theology of Hair (Menna Elfyn, in *Welsh Women's Poetry*, 296).

Diarmuid Johnson

*CE: Common Era, a non-sectarian form for AD

** *The Bloodaxe Book of Modern Welsh Poetry* (eds. M. Elfyn, J. Rowlands) Bloodaxe 2003

English-language fiction from Wales

Abse, Dannie

There Was a Young Man from Cardiff

Abse's book is an unusual mixture of short stories and diaristic pieces along with a few examples of his poetry, the form of writing he is best known for. As the book largely has a family focus we inevitably meet some larger-than-life members of a Welsh–Jewish family, like Uncle Eddie the dodgy entrepreneur ('count your teeth. . . after you've seen Eddie') as well as more ordinary family members in their larger-than-life moments.

The frequent humorous passages of *There Was a Young Man from Cardiff* (which follows on from a related work *Ash on a Young Man's Sleeve*) are often shaded by Chekhovian darkness as menace and mystery slide out of the ordinary like the mist rising from the sea at Abse's beloved Ogmore (a village between Cardiff and Swansea) where many of the pieces are set. In this and other ways he derives profundity from small matters and the extraordinariness of the ordinary, very much in the manner of the contemporary poetry of the time. One of the things Abse is very good at is recognising how individuality develops or even festers with age and most of his characters are middle aged or older. Characters like Gene Harvey, the literary flaneur and all-round nuisance, or Wyn Phillips, a returned exile whose return has been only to a melancholy, perhaps fatal detachment in the gentle world of Ogmore-by-Sea or the ghostly fisherman, Evans, who is supposedly half-Welsh, half-Red Indian — all achieve a tremendous solidity in the reader's mind and somehow a desire to like them is born, however awful they seem. Perhaps Abse's other career as doctor lent him insights into the later human condition rare amongst writers.

At his very best, as in the brief but funny little eyeful about the end of World War Two entitled '1945: Bridgend, Glamorgan', Abse is just perfect. RK

❱❱ My Uncle Isidore was a distant foreign relative, not always distant. He was connected to our family by marriage. This lemon-tea Bolshevik, who never did any work, visited members of the family from time to time. Once, my cousin Adam Shepherd had asked him what he did every day. 'Nothing,' Uncle Isidore had replied. 'And I don't do that until after lunch.' 43

That June evening when Wyn Phillips first called on us, only my wife, my mother and I were there. I had been in Cardiff to record a Dial a Poem earlier and, back at Ogmore, I told my mother that if she wished to hear me read it, all she had to do was dial a certain Cardiff number. She stood in the hall, the telephone receiver next to her ear, while I dialled the numerals for her. 'I haven't heard you read your poetry for twenty years,' she complained. I leaned towards her and the telephone receiver to ensure that the correct dialling tone sounded. I heard a click, a woman briefly introducing me and then my own voice reading a poem. My mother (in 1975 she was eighty-five years old) stood very still, listening, concentrating. Then she-bellowed into the phone, 'Speak up, son'. **‹‹** 167

Azzopardi, Trezza

The Hiding Place

Set in the old Cardiff docklands of Tiger Bay, Trezza Azzopardi's Booker shortlisted novel *The Hiding Place* is the story of Maltese immigrant Frank Gauci, his Welsh wife Mary, and their six daughters: Celesta, Marina, Rose, Fran, Luca, and Dolores. Through the eyes of the youngest daughter, Dolores or Dol, a vivid picture of Cardiff's seedy 1960s underworld is painted: its vibrant immigrant community of gangsters, gaming rooms and betting shops, cafés, clubs and back-to-back terraces. But Azzopardi's main focus is the troubled family life of the Gaucis themselves, the harrowing memories of abuse, deprivation and loss that, even thirty years on, refuse to fade for Dolores and are brought sharply into relief when, after three decades of absence, she returns to Cardiff on the news of her mother's death. Confronted once more with her troubled past, Dolores finds herself locked in a struggle with both the willed amnesia of her sisters and her own uncertain memories — not to mention the literal erasure of place by Cardiff's dockland developers — to salvage from this past something meaningful for the future. To what extent she succeeds in this is a question that the novel's wonderfully ambivalent ending refuses to answer definitively.

The legacy and dynamics of abuse are portrayed here with empathy and insight. Frankie's brutal wielding of power over his family is contrasted with his inability to stand up to gangster Joe Medora and his sense of powerlessness outside the home seems to fuel his violent temper within it. The different ways in which Dolores' sisters react to their experience of abuse and its effect on the development of their personalities is convincingly conveyed. While Frankie's violent behaviour is replicated in Rose and Luca's bullying of Dol, and, in the case of Fran, turned inwards upon herself in acts of self-harming, Celesta, the eldest of Frankie's daughters, becomes obsessed with presenting a front of sober respectability and rigid self-control — one which conceals, even from herself, the absence of any real control over her own life.

For Dolores, the impact of abuse, neglect, the breakdown of her mother, and the eventual dissolution of the family when she is only five, is conveyed literally and metaphorically by the powerful symbol of her missing left hand, lost in a fire when she was still a baby. Azzopardi traces this accident to Frankie's selfishness and negligence, which drive his wife to distraction and even force her into prostituting herself to her creditors.

By locating the fire in the context of Frankie's abusive relationship with his family, Azzopardi transforms Dol's missing hand into a metaphor symptomatic of her father's destructive influence while simultaneously performing a broader symbolic role as the physical expression of Dolores' psychological mutilation. In a powerful image, it is Dolores herself who makes the comparison, as she likens the loss of mother, sisters and home to the phantom pains of her absent limb.

The Hiding Place contains a very bleak vision of human relationships, albeit there is some humour in Dolores' satirical view of adult foibles, while the sisters' verbal exchanges are also comically charged, if sometimes painfully so. Whichever way we interpret the novel's ending, the beauty of Azzopardi's writing transcends bleakness, as, with poetic brevity, she shapes Dolores' past into a purposeful structure — her sustained quest to find meaning. HR

)) Frankie strolls past the Bute Street cafes, nodding now and again at a familiar face, or raising his hatted hand in a greeting. This is Frankie's patch. Most of the restaurants and cafes are owned and run by his friends: seamen from the Tramp Trade who came to rest and stopped for good. And my father has also stopped, for now, although like most of the other Maltese, he won't settle in the city — he can't escape the salt-scent of the docks. When he talks about his ship coming in, meaning a winning streak, an odds-on favourite, a dead cert, he also feels, like glitter in his blood, the day when he will take a folded stash of money and simply disappear.

This is not that day. This is the day I am burnt. **((24**

Barnie, John

Ice

John Barnie is a polymath, seemingly rather good at everything. Not only is he editor of the important Welsh cultural magazine *Planet*, he is also a poet, essayist (particularly on politics and the environment) and blues musician, and in his latest work he brings these various talents together for the first time. *Ice* is a novel in verse — but don't let that put you off. Thankfully, it lacks those qualities we tend to associate with 'traditional' poetry: it is not flowery or pretentious; it is not difficult for the sake of it; it doesn't rhyme. It is, instead, surprisingly readable and extremely effective, conveying both a sense of place and the hopes and fears of the main characters with a richness and economy impossible to achieve through conventional prose. And what is there here of Barnie's blues-playing side? Far from this being the lamentations of a broke drifter whose wife leaves him and takes the dog, *Ice* is a vision of an apocalyptic future in which global warming has precipitated a new ice age and humanity is on the brink of self-destruction. Now, that's the blues...

The events described in the run-up to the 'Great Cold' are disturbingly familiar: retreating glaciers, floods and extreme weather. To date (2008), global warming has already melted an area of Siberian permafrost larger than France and Germany combined and recent years have seen unprecedented levels of flooding in Europe and Asia and enormous destruction in New Orleans.

Recounted in retrospect through folktales told by 'The Storyteller' or archive film shown in the 'VideoDome', such events are shown to be unmistakable precursors of the ecological devastation that in the future world of the novel has reduced the earth to a barren, icy wasteland. Most poignant and prescient of all, however, is the description of a piece of historical film in which shaky hand-held amateur camcorder footage captures a giant wave, 'swinging up and up/ smooth-riding gathering its power, silent and positive,/ rearing towards the islands that we can no longer see behind us'. *Ice* was first published in 2001 — three years before the Boxing Day tsunami killed some two hundred thousand people around the Indian Ocean. Coincidence, or an astonishing prediction?

Ice deals not with this monumental environmental disaster itself but with the human consequences of its aftermath. It is five generations since the onset of the 'Great Cold', when a lucky few were selected for survival whilst out on the frozen tundra the countless masses of the Abandoned were left to perish. The descendants of those survivors live in Banda, a subterranean city of caves and tunnels carved deep in the rock. Holed up underground like worms or rats, life is hard. There is little of beauty and the harsh conditions are exacerbated by the suicidal warmongering of the presiding totalitarian regime. Having launched an unprovoked attack on a neighbouring tunnel-dwelling community, the Nekton, Banda awaits the inevitable reprisal.

So is it all doom and gloom? Well, not entirely. Even in the cold and darkness of this inhospitable environment, there are pockets of warmth, glimmers of hope. Against the odds, life and love bloom, if only briefly. *Ice's* main protagonist, a soldier, falls for Galathea, a woman who embodies all those qualities suppressed by the increasingly brutal authorities — compassion, imagination, creativity. Together they plant a precious packet of seeds that had been handed down to Galathea through the generations; though most of the seeds fail to germinate, the wild marigolds flower for a few weeks, a fleeting flash of colour in an otherwise grey world. This is no sentimental love story, however. We know there can be only one possible outcome for Galathea and her lover, as for all the citizens of Banda. Caught like rats in a trap, there can be no escaping humanity's appetite for destruction, both of the earth and of itself.

A conscious reworking of *1984*, Barnie has replaced Orwell's nightmare with a vision of a future that is perhaps even worse. *Ice* is elegant, intelligent and unashamedly political, a powerful package. CP

)) Here they come, we can see them far out over the snow

gliding like wraiths, the ice become nervous and alive;

through binoculars you can see how busy they are,

officers veering round, keeping formation,

the troops powering themselves hard with left-right strokes of their ski-sticks

the cold black nose of an automatic jogging on their backs;

we wait in our slit trenches of ice; it cannot be that they have not seen us;

yet they come on; and behind them another wave and another behind that,

bobbing with the effort, the left-right of the ski sticks powering them on;

we wait... wait... under a grey sky in the ice;

[...]

I squeeze the trigger in a two-second burst

and the lead officer flips on his back, a foot and a ski turn over once, and he is still;

all along the line the rapid bursts of fire, the advance guard

slipping to the snow as if all the while they had not been real

and bullets had made the genie go out of them;

but the next line comes on, and I can see another wave, and another, beyond them;

what is death, goes the old Nekton song,

but a pat on the back from a long-lost friend. **((** 144

Barry, Desmond

A Bloody Good Friday

1977. The Queen's silver jubilee; skinheads; punk; high unemployment; civil and industrial unrest; the year of the four-month-long bread strike in south Wales. Storm clouds are gathering above Merthyr, a (soon to be former) mining town already in sharp decline. Against this backdrop, Davey Daunt, known in the pre-politically correct environment of the 1970s Welsh valleys as 'Spazzy' on account of a leg withered by polio, recounts the intertwined stories of a number of dodgy local characters as their paths cross, re-cross and finally badly entangle in the late hours of one fateful and extremely bloody Good Friday.

Macky, Davey's best mate, released from prison just that morning, is out, along with fellow hard cases Morgan and Gerry, to paint the town red. Blood red. Bunyan, Davey's childhood abuser, heads towards the high street curryhouse in a drunken stupor. In the ghetto that is the notorious Gurnos housing estate, Gripper, the leader of a gang of skinheads known as the Shop Boys, is arrested and his second-in-command, keen to prove his yobbish credentials, steps in with a rallying cry of anarchy and recreational violence. He leads the delinquent mob on a rampage down to the town, leaving a trail of up-ended rubbish bins, broken glass and bloodied victims in their wake. There is a palpable tension in the air that, like the 'thick Welsh accents' of the hooligan Shop Boys, you could cut with a knife — 'if they didn't cut you first'. And it's all about to kick off. . .

In the Rails pub, The Clash's *White Riot* is playing on the jukebox. In a world where even small details seem to take on prophetic significance, this is not a good sign. In fact, the novel is teeming with signs, omens and portents (the taxi that stops for Davey and comrades has the number plate AHB 666K), even gypsy curses, and all these contribute to the sense of impending doom well before Macky sets off on his kamikaze Kawasaki ride. Call it coincidence, fate, karma or divine retribution, there is the suggestion that supernatural forces are at work in the intricate machinations that contrive to bring all these elements together in a crescendo of chaos. Perhaps it was Macky's ill-advised decision to attempt a headstand within striking distance of three gypsies in the bar of the Wellington that started the ball rolling (and the blood flowing). Or possibly it was the stone that Gripper lobbed at Police Constable Phillips' panda patrol car. Or maybe, somewhere over Merthyr, a butterfly flapped its wings. Whatever the spark that lit the blue touchpaper on the night's explosive proceedings, a chain of events is set in motion that builds inexorably to a bloody conclusion. Chaos theory may or may not explain how each apparently insignificant event plays a vital role in the ensuing tragedy, but one thing's for certain: chaos ensues.

Unlike the harsh violence and its brain-dead perpetrators, however, *A Bloody Good Friday* itself is not mindless or gratuitous. It is a provocative and complex meditation on the nature of heroism and on machismo, masculinity and its mythos. A word of warning, though: this is an unflinching examination of the ugly underbelly of society. Sexually explicit and graphically gory (with a good poke of bad language), this is not for the easily offended. However, if you do have the constitution for it and appreciate the work of Irvine Welsh or Niall Griffiths, then join in the fun. CP

)) What, you may ask, is Welsh about this mam with her Virgins and Val Doonicans? Should she not be chapel? And speak Cymraeg*? Well, where else does she belong? Born and bred in Merthyr. And Maeve had never been out of Merthyr until she was twenty-four and went on her honeymoon to London. Who defines Welsh? Richard Llewellyn? How green was my f***ing valley? Gimme a break. Spend a bit of time in the Gurnos, or on the Ely Estate in Cardiff, or in Tiger Bay. F*** it, even Shirley Bassey's black. **((66**

*The Welsh word for the Welsh language

Berry, Ron

So Long, Hector Bebb

Ron Berry's vivid, often brutal novel tells the story of a fictional British Champion boxer, Hector Bebb, whose life is unravelled by violence. A snapshot of 1960s Cymmer in south Wales (complete with dialects) where the people are hard-working, hard-drinking, and hard-fighting, the novel traces the effects of violence and savagery — that which is legitimised by war and that by the boxing ring, as well as that which is not tolerated at all in civilised society.

We join Hector in training for his comeback bout, following a year-long suspension for biting an opponent. His story is told through a variety of perspectives — as well as Hector's voice, there are thirteen other narrators including his wife, his trainer, his manager and other amateur boxers, past and present. Woven into the story of his preparations therefore are memories of how Hector started to box, accounts of fights through the years, and an exploration of the relationships of those connected to Hector and the other members of the White Hart Boxing club.

Hector's obsessive preparations pay off, as he wins the British Champion Middleweight title. But the following night Hector's fists rob him of glory as he punches, and kills, Emlyn Winton, his wife's lover. With the police looking for him, he says 'So Long, Hector Bebb', adopts a new identity and becomes an outlaw like the heroes of the pulp cowboy novels he reads. The violence of the boxing ring is replaced by the savagery of survival on the hills above Cymmer and Tosteg. This existence is made increasingly difficult as the landscape is undergoing a process of industrialisation and taming itself, by the planting of swathes of Forestry Commission conifers.

The juxtaposition of the acceptable violence of the boxing ring with the Coldra Café punch-up is startling, and Berry uses it to reveal the fragility of social conditioning. Reactions to the assault are divided — but no-one condemns the violent act; some characters believe that Hector should have struck his wife instead, while others think the act was legitimate husbandly revenge. Each character, however, sees violence as the only solution. The reader is encouraged to question this standpoint through the portrayal of victims of 'legitimate' violence, most significantly Mel Carpenter, a boxer left brain-damaged after losing a fight to Hector, and Prince Jenkin Saddler, a maimed war veteran, physically and psychologically scarred by his experience of battle. Both are now distanced from society — one in a mental hospital, the other by his solitary existence farming on the hills.

In Hector's situation, the reactions of the community, the haunting memories of a war veteran and the violence of the boxing ring, Berry illuminates the fine line that separates the supposedly civilised from the savage and demonstrates the fragility and hollowness of social conditioning. The barely cloaked greed, neediness and lasciviousness of many of the characters reveal that Hector is not the only 'trained animal' in Cymmer. SM

)) 'Sammy John found him. No argument. Sammy's paid obligation to bring him on. Earned income vide our Clause Four. Myself and Bebb, we're direct opposites. He makes his own rulings. Typical jungle master type. He'll last out ten, fifteen years. Beautiful timing. Coordination very sharp. One of our Rolls Royce fighters. Thrown and bred for the title. We'll get there when he's fully mature. Say four, five more years, give or take re the opposition in the running. My prediction. Exactly. Gamble on that. I mean to say, putting the drop on Len Jules. Just a ragged arsed kid. Trust him? By God, trust Hector Bebb? Uh? Sammy? True, true, no-one but Sammy. Me, I trust Sammy John. He idolises that boy. Fathers him. Right, all right. Who's objecting? Young Bebb's short of a real dad. The old mother, she reared him on the parish. Charity and Parish. That's no shame in my eyes'. **((** 23–4

Bush, Duncan

Glass Shot

Glass Shot is the unalloyed and unrelieved portrait of a sociopath, a man who, while apparently conforming to social norms in his lifestyle and appearance, lacks the crucial inner behavioural regulator of empathy for others.

As Bush drags us into the mind of this self-centred and ignorant man whose family ties and social pride have been severed by marriage breakdown — his wife, much to his disgust, has left him for a teacher, the better to indulge middle-class cottagey-décor and Volvo-driving aspirations — we begin to feel bullied by this angry and threatening pub-bore type. His chronic anxiety and existential misery fester in the bleak universe constituted by the tyre-fitters' where he works, his porno consumption, sex fantasies, ideas of revenge and gambling activities. His fantasy life in fact folds in and out of his consciousness and Bush succeeds in getting us to follow these twists to understand how he gradually oversteps the line from solipsistic resentment to vicious fantasy-driven behaviour against others when he kidnaps a girl. He then demonstrates a kind of perverse self-deceiving innocence in his lack of understanding of the reality he will induce by this act.

This all builds to an engaging menace in the last part of the book, although whether this is pleasurable beyond entertainment or distraction value depends on the reader enjoying a wholly negative portrayal of human nature; doesn't this imply a degree of self-hatred for ourselves? Or perhaps we should appreciate *Glass Shot* as insightful morality tale and social critique of the brutalised inner desert of a hackneyed masculinity revolving around thoughts of leather jackets, 'gorgeous blondes', flash motors, weight training and TV shows. RK

)) Then, right at the head of the valley, is a place I remember and I know I'm almost at the end of the road. It's only one more dirty-looking, Welsh, played-out little village, don't even ask me to pronounce the fucking name of it. Just another place that grew up around a hole in the ground twenty miles from nowhere, a couple of dozen or so houses, every one complete with outside toilets, and views of half-grassed slagheaps if you take a glance out of the wrong window. **((** 66

Burke, Sean

Deadwater

Sean Burke's striking debut novel is set in Cardiff's notorious Butetown district in 1989, prior to the massive redevelopment which transformed that part of the Welsh capital. An urban thriller in the tradition of George Pelecanos and James Lee Burke, *Deadwater* begins with the gruesome murder of prostitute Christina Villers. Pharmacist and alcoholic Jack Farissey wakes the next morning, covered in blood and with no memory of the previous night. What follows is an odyssey into an anarchic world of pool halls, seedy pubs and rundown cafés, a blighted place of poverty, drug abuse, prostitution and gang violence.

Jack Farissey is complex, morally ambiguous and contradictory: at once negligent and protective, selfish and compassionate, he provides handouts of medicine to needy locals, recreationally consumes some of his stock himself and occasionally writes papers for pharmacological journals. A Butetown native made good, Farissey's pregnant lover Victoria has recently returned from studying law in London to take up a job with dubious local solicitors Madieson and Madieson. Since she has also been engaged in an apparently open affair with Jack's childhood friend, dissolute musician Jess Simmonds, the paternity of her unborn child is unclear.

Prompted by Detective Inspector Loudon Hargest of the local police, an officer with a lifelong association with Butetown and its residents, Farissey, Simmonds, and prostitute Lida Varaillon give statements implicating feared Butetown gangsters Carl and Tony Baja in the murder. Madieson and Madieson are engaged as the Bajas' defence, and it is Victoria who is assigned to the case. It is not long before the Bajas are acquitted and, to the horror of those who betrayed them, allowed to go free. "'I wasn't there when my boy said his first sentences," Carl Baja tells the TV news on his release. "There's some people in Butetown should suffer like I did.'"

Those with most reason to fear are Lida Varaillon, who falsely claimed to have witnessed Christina's murder at the hands of the Bajas, as well as Jess Simmonds and Farissey himself, whose statement, given under hypnosis, is transcribed by Burke as an ambiguous, blood-soaked stream-of-consciousness. Upon the brothers' release, Lida Varaillon is provided with a safe house in Bristol by Hargest. Jess Simmonds, meanwhile, goes on the run to escape the Bajas' retribution. When Farissey and Victoria go to Simmonds' former home, they find a series of gruesome keepsakes from women he has slept with, including Victoria. On their return to their own home they discover that the place has been broken in to and copies of Victoria's legal papers stolen — papers which detail the precise extent of Farissey's role in the Bajas' arrest.

It is not long before Farissey is visited by the Bajas — "'We won't put a mark on you,'" they promise — and forced to accompany them to Bristol, where, with Farissey's help, they intend to find and punish Lida Varaillon. Returning to Cardiff without success, they keep their promise to Farissey, force-feeding him with drugs.

There follows a grim denouement culminating in a scene of memorable horror; a fitting finale to a novel peopled by characters who seek light in the darkness but are continually thwarted by circumstances.

Deadwater is both skilfully plotted thriller and social critique, a book that rises above the commonplace. What really thrills though is Burke's facility with language — every sentence leads the reader further into the hellish underbelly of a Cardiff depicted with poetic finesse. WA

)) It would be like taking the road to Damascus backwards, a dawn recomposed by the building, brewing night. To never see in skies anything but imprecations and treachery, or hear the chatter of birds without hearing also a whirring fury of omens in his own head. He would burn on and out, burn in the single hope that these electric storms of Christ and Kali be finally quelled, the dramas come to fruition on a birthday, an intersection of roads, or a car's iconic numberplate and himself then be gone, buried, drowned, whatever, and vindicated. **((** 156

Collins, Richard

The Land as Viewed from the Sea

The Land as Viewed from the Sea is Richard Collins' remarkable debut novel. It is an unconventional love story that pushes the limits of language and form to capture the complexity of memory and loss. Its prologue sets the background for the whole novel, invoking an expanse of grey-green sea constantly in flux. The waves journey onwards with previously felt forces, present momentum and the promise of future encounters. From this seemingly limitless fluidity the narrative shifts to an interior landscape to focus on a man and a woman arguing.

This stylised opening sequence could not be more in contrast to the earthy reality of rural life with which the story begins. Two men work companionably in the fields, one after an absence of some years. The latter, John, the ostensible 'author', is invigorated by the effect the natural environment has upon his senses; his awareness of physical reality has been dulled by his residence in the city and some of the novel's most vivid and lyrical passages stem from his renewed receptivity to nature.

Photographer and artist, John is preoccupied by a different artistic medium, his 'cheap hobby' of writing a one-off novel. His friend Julian, the slightly aloof but kindly organic farmer, becomes a ready patron for this venture and an unwilling, if curiously engaged, first reader. The lines blur between fiction and reality, past and present, as it is revealed that Julian's growing appetite for the fledgling fiction is far from disinterested.

The Land as Viewed from the Sea is also the title of John's novel and symbolic of the shifting perspectives and changing visions of reality that are Collins' central concerns. The sea, a nurturing yet destructive force, represents a fusion of infinite inventiveness with self-absorption.

The novel, like the sea, repeats patterns and there are several passages that are re-worked and re-presented. Subtle changes are often inserted to enforce the idea that it is not possible to capture or define human relationships from only one viewpoint.

Excerpts from John's novel appear in the text as piecemeal offerings for Julian to comment upon. This text-within-a-text relates the story of a past love affair. There are two distinct vantage points. In the first, a nameless man sails around an undisclosed coastline, remembering his past according to the memories the landscape evokes from a distance. "'He hadn't planned this but he has a startlingly clear vision of her face in front of him. He doesn't need this. All around him the water is dark and inhospitable.'"

The second narrative is grittier and told from within the relationship: "'And you're never selfish?" she asks. "You never put yourself first? Get real please'.'

He sits on the sofa and sulks. He doesn't want this to be happening. She distracts herself by tidying the room and he watches her'.

The complexities of love and sexuality are captured with subtlety and the dreamlike effect of the whole novel is created by constant changes in style and focus. Collins emphasises the transient nature of human interaction with this method of constant narrative movement. Disillusionment and deception tarnish this 'strange world of lovers, exaggeratedly focussed on each other, oblivious of the world around them'. Pleasure and pain co-exist in this play of emotions, by turns intense, passionate, beautiful but also obsessive, destructive and dangerous.

The distinct, yet inextricable, narratives begin to merge with the creative act of writing that frames the work. Autobiography is confused with fiction and the novel escapes from the pages into the 'real' world. Julian, the reader, becomes writer, naming the previously unnamed characters. And it becomes clear that John, the would-be novelist, has previously denied identification with his art as a deliberate act of self-preservation. 'It's changed and distorted but maybe somewhere, in its essence, it is about me'.

The effect of these different stories combined makes this a haunting work. Collins succeeds in producing a narrative reflecting many aspects of human relationships and reveals the fragility and beauty inherent in them. SRR

) I have my eyes shut again. It's a good way to hold a conversation, just the sound of our own and someone else's voices. I can't see the expression on Julian's face so I have a certain freedom to say what I want. The confessional must be like this — two anonymous voices, no eye contact. But now, as ever, we will both hold back as much as we say. I hope.

'All these months of working together and you still won't ask about her,' Julian says.

'There's a real person we don't talk about'.

'I think that's best for me'.

[...]

The sun goes behind a cloud and I can feel a cool breeze on my skin. I have to open my eyes and put my t-shirt on.

'Why does the wind pick up when the sun goes behind a cloud?' I ask. 'I don't understand'.

'The wind doesn't pick up, it's just that you can't feel it when the heat of the sun is on your skin. It's changed perception'. He looks at me and grins.

'That's the sort of thing you're interested in, isn't it?' **‹‹** 152–3

Davies, Stevie

The Element of Water

The twin narratives of *The Element of Water* take place in 1945 and 1958. Following Hitler's suicide in the last days of World War Two in Europe, Admiral Dönitz is pronounced head of state, and establishes the headquarters of the shattered Reich at Ruhleben naval camp on Lake Plön. As the Allies approach, Dönitz's remaining forces flee, throwing their medals and weapons into the lake's dark waters. Thirteen years later, the building has become a British forces boarding school (which, we are told in a foreword, the author herself attended). Michael Quantz, a former Nazi intelligence officer based at Ruhleben during Dönitz's time, and his adult son Wolfi are now music teachers at the British school. Both men are haunted — Wolfi by the death of his mother during an allied air raid, his father by the atrocities he witnessed during the war, particularly those perpetrated by his childhood friend Paul Dahl: 'From a seraphic Lutheran chorister, Paul had ripened to the purest filth'. Wolfi, a shy, awkward young man, struggles with the burgeoning contempt he and his peers have for the complicity of his father's generation. The gulf between father and son widens further when young teacher Isolde ('Issie') Dahl arrives at the school from Britain, where she had been living in Swansea with her German mother, Renate, and her timid Welsh stepfather, Owen.

The school is run by Mr Patterson, an authoritarian with a colonialist streak and an unwholesome admiration for Admiral Dönitz — as well as a collection of Nazi memorabilia in his office salvaged from Lake Plön. Issie is shocked by the brutality of Patterson's regime, by the indifference of some of her fellow teachers, and the callousness of the children themselves. When she tries to prevent the bullying of one particular pupil, Rachel, she is thwarted by both the apathy of her colleagues and the anti-Semitism of the children's German matron.

Slowly, as Issie and Wolfi fall in love, the truth of her parentage begins to emerge. "'My father disowned me," she says. "Then we disown him," Wolfi replies'. The novel climaxes when Rachel goes missing and, while out searching for her, Issie and Michael encounter a nearby reunion of former Nazi officials. When Rachel's body is discovered in the lake, Issie is racked with guilt, knowing that she could have done more for the child had she not been so consumed by her new love. Ultimately, Renate confesses the secret she has kept from her daughter all her life, and Issie and Wolfi return to Swansea, prompting a confrontation which finally forces Renate to reconcile herself with the ghosts of the past.

In this novel about guilt, responsibility and the intractability of the past, Stevie Davies proves herself to be one of Wales' subtlest yet most strikingly lyrical writers. Eschewing an easy resolution she guides the reader through a plot of great moral and narrative complexity with skill, ever eager to sensitise us to the echoes of history, and to the humanity which can be found even in those capable of the most inhumane acts. WA

)) A girl unloosed lank hair, which tumbled down her back from its roll, and, singing, suddenly pulled her blouse up over her head in one lithe movement. Stop it, just stop that rude nonsense, the mother grumbled feebly, a token resistance, because decency takes a while to die and you have to say something. But the girl's bared breasts caught the light and Michael's eye; he braked, mesmerised to watch her brief rapturous dance, arms gracefully extended, whirling on the spot. And singing. Mind gone, he presumed, raped or whatever, along the way. Come on, Effi, put your things back on, the mother pleaded. Be a good girl for Mummy. And she stopped, staggered disorientated and, catching Quantz's eye, flashed him a smile that would have been tearingly beautiful; would have been, except that her teeth were entirely gone. **((** 3

Evans, Caradoc

My People

Hailed as the father of 'Anglo-Welsh' literature, Caradoc Evans rose to notoriety with this controversial first collection, *My People*. First published in 1915, the fifteen stories are all set in the fictional village of Manteg and are also unified by recurring themes and characters. The stories depict a rural, Welsh-speaking and religiously Nonconformist community peopled by half-wits, social misfits, lecherous misogynists and oppressive Methodist ministers, all of whom share an obsessive and hollow materialism. Their motto is 'keep your purse full and the strings tight, and nothing will fail you'.

Each story is set within the dominant institution of the place, Capel Sion ('Zion Chapel'), ruled with self-interest and sham respectability by the chapel elders and the revered ministers 'as important as God' — and who have the biggest farms to boot. The stories are a merciless, unflinching attack on the parochialism and hypocrisy of the religious establishment as seen by Evans. The narrative voice, with its strong biblical cadence and its cold objectivity, reinforces his satire.

In *My People* religion is used cynically to maintain the social hierarchy. The chapel retails a shallow faith that measures its preachers by the 'hwyl' or moving eloquence they demonstrate in the pulpit on a Sunday. This is fiercely satirised, for example in the story 'The Talent thou Gavest' with Eben's diminishing stature as a minister evident in the fact that 'no one wept again'.

This is also a vindictive and malevolent society, almost absurdly bleak, with few redeeming features. One of the few decent folk of Manteg, the self-sacrificing Nanni, is found dead, her face eaten away by rats. Even this grotesque occurrence enforces the natural order — Nanni is living off poor relief and has little to offer the wealthy rulers of the chapel authority, or Seiat. The treatment of women in this world is indeed particularly brutal. In the story 'A Heifer without Blemish' a man's search for a wife is a transaction comparable to the purchase of a healthy beast. In fact, the latter negotiation takes more of his time and attention.

All of the stories demonstrate a similar attitude. Women are viewed as either a commodity or a wasteful burden on the male. The female, at various times referred to as 'dirty clod', 'bitch', 'hussy', 'concubine' and 'temptress', is an inferior to be exploited and abused.

When a man cannot control his lust for a woman, she is inevitably seen as the instigator. Witness the horrifying incestuous rape of Matilda, who at the end of one story is driven like an animal to the local madhouse. Shockingly, the chapel rally behind her father, encouraged by the Respected* Davydd-Bern Davydd because 'his free will offerings to the Temple are generous'.

On first publication *My People* thrilled with its originality and inventive use of non-standard English. Combining an exhilarating blend of realism and fantasy, emphasised by the contrast between the cold and dispassionate narrative stance and the often grotesque representation of character, Evans created a dazzling portrait of peasant backwardness across the border. His audience, a middle-class English readership, revelled in the moral and intellectual inferiority of the Welsh whose language and culture Evans exploited so mercilessly to create his fictional world.

Evans used the 'original' language of his countrymen, translating idioms and syntax literally and in so doing capitalised on the differing word order and allusions this created when writing in English. The rich dialect of Cardiganshire

Welsh as morphed into English renders his characters inarticulate and ridiculous yet headily poetic with expressions such as 'sober serious', 'head stiff', 'Big Man', 'little father' — phrases natural in the source language but seemingly farcical in a translated foreign tongue. His design was to convey difference and to emphasise the depravity of this world. Distortion of language becomes a means of artistic expression. In directly transposing from one language to another the dialogue can at times be difficult to follow. But in his inversions and biblical inflections Evans created a medium rich in linguistic play that was admired by many of his contemporaries, most notably Joyce, who went on to manipulate the English language to further extremes. SRR

*'Respected' was used as a religious title in the Welsh-speaking community portrayed by Evans.

)) The Sabbath came, and people on their way to Capel Sion saw William Jenkins go up the narrow Roman road to Penrhos, and they said one to another: 'Close will be the bargaining'. Simon was glad that Sara Jane had found favour in William's eyes: here was a godly man and one of substance; he owned a Shop General*, his coat was always dry, and he wore a collar every day in the week, and he received many red pennies in the course of a day. Simon took him out on the moor.

'Shall we talk this business then at once?' Mishtir Jenkins observed. 'Make plain Sara Jane's inheritance'.

'Much, little boy'.

'Penrhos will come to Sara Jane, then?'

'Iss, man'.

'Right that is, Simon. Wealthy am I. Do I not own Shop General? Man bach, there's a grand business for you!' **((** 'The Way of the Earth' 68.

* 'general store'

Griffiths, Niall

Grits

Grits was Liverpool-born Niall Griffiths' first novel and establishes the fictional world in which all his novels to date — *Sheepshagger, Kelly and Victor, Stump* and *Wreckage* — have been located. When first published, this tale of 1990s drug culture and social decay in a Welsh seaside resort (Griffiths' adopted home of Aberystwyth) naturally inspired comparisons with Irvine Welsh's *Trainspotting*, a similarly-themed novel set in Edinburgh. Certainly, both novels focus on those deemed marginal by the rest of society, down-and-outs whose consumption of drugs and alcohol is portrayed as a displaced revolt against consumerist values.

Grits also follows *Trainspotting* in adopting a multiple, vernacular narrative (Griffiths deploys eleven first-person narrators) that lets its characters speak directly to the reader. However, it would be unfair on Griffiths to overstress the similarities. Griffiths' treatment of his material differs considerably from that of Welsh and the dominant motif of his work — the pursuit of metaphysical meaning and order in a disordered and meaningless world — owes more to the American novelist Cormac McCarthy than to any British-based author.

This is not a novel for the squeamish. The late twentieth century collapse of religious belief and the absence of structure in the characters' lives is registered in *Grits* in the form of the scatological and the bodily grotesque — in language that will doubtless turn many readers' stomachs! Foregrounding the apparent chaos of the body and its processes, Griffiths' characters (in particular Colm) reflect the extent to which concepts such as the taboo and the sacred no longer hold, and are thus no longer able to order life's chaotic physicality. The response of both characters and the novel to this collapse of metaphysical meaning is very ambivalent and, not surprisingly, is echoed in the ambivalence of their attitudes towards the grotesque, which throughout the novel is both embraced with libertarian glee and recoiled from with horror and disgust. Indeed, for the novel's characters, the grotesque's transgressive qualities come to symbolise not only freedom from social, moral and religious constraints, but also the ultimate meaninglessness of biological existence.

It is drink, sex and drugs that seem to offer, initially at least, a way out of this existential dilemma. Although Griffiths does not flinch from portraying the sordid and destructive reality of substance abuse, he is also at pains to describe the other side of drug use, its promise (however tantalising and fleeting) of freedom and transcendence. Drink, drugs and sexual promiscuity are figured in almost spiritual terms within the novel, their pleasures delineated in a language metaphysical in its quality and intensity. Ultimately, however, Griffiths' portrayal of drug culture adopts the same ambivalence present in his depiction of the grotesque. If drugs offer, on the one hand, a sublime jouissance that nothing else can match, they only do so by opening the self out to a terrifying awareness of its physical vulnerability. Drugs, the novel suggests, 'show yew yer own death'; they reveal in stark relief the fragility of the boundaries that guard one's transient existence from the chaos threatening always to overwhelm it.

Griffiths is undoubtedly a gifted writer and despite the abject horrors it is used to express his language has a lyric quality that reflects his characters' anguished yearning for stability and meaning. While some readers may feel that not all of Griffiths's 'voices' are equally successful, and that the novel itself is a little overlong, *Grits* nevertheless remains a scintillating piece of writing, a unique and powerful contribution to Wales' literature in English. HR

)) Memories. . . like a shelterin thicket ter hide within. A defence mechanism an al tell yer fuckin why; cos nothing ever prepares yer fer this horror, nothin can ever help yer ter build up thee emotional defences yer need ter deal with the shite an terror inherent in this life, this werld, cos the shite an the terror ar too fuckin big, too huge and horrendous too shitey and too terrible ter ever be fuckin coped with, they'll eat you in one gulp and shit yer out bifore yuv ad time ter shed yer ferst fuckin tear. Ther's nothin yer can do. NOTHING. An if ther's nowt after death then why be afraid uv it? That makes sense, dunnit? But the thought uv tha nothingness, tha void, tha vacuum, adds horror and trembling an meaninglessness to the something tha precedes it, the life. . . **((** 326

Gwyn, Richard

The Colour of a Dog Running Away

1990s Barcelona, a surreal and postmodern landscape peopled by rooftop raiders, English teachers, artists and fire-eaters. A city that is both menacing and inspirational. The majority of the narrative takes place in the atmospheric Gothic quarter with its narrow alleyways, medieval churches, hidden squares and shady bars, the latter frequented with zealous regularity by the improbably named Rhys Morgan Aurelio Lucas and his displaced friends.

Lucas is a thirty-three-year old translator and aspiring musician whose story begins with his witnessing a mugging one May evening. The next day a mysterious postcard arrives leading him to the beautiful Barcelonesa, Nuria, with whom he begins an intensely passionate affair.

Nuria seems to provide Lucas with stability and meaning in a world of fleeting attachments and constant movement. But nothing is as it seems in this city where the 'abiding attraction lies in its relentless powers of reinvention, a ruthless creativity that rubs off on people after the briefest visit'.

The plot takes an unexpected turn when the couple are kidnapped by an ancient religious sect bent on solving a seven-hundred-year-old mystery. The Cathars, described here as nature-loving ascetic Christians, were persecuted as heretics during the Catholic Middle Ages. Lucas finds himself implicated in medieval treachery and the fate of seventeen disappeared souls. The mark of the yellow cross, age-old symbol of religious unorthodoxy, attains ambiguous significance with the revival of this religion in a mountain hideaway in contemporary Catalonia.

Held captive and separated from Nuria, Lucas finds himself doubting his own existence as memory and personal history are literally occupied by a powerful external force. Personal liberty is tested as the self-appointed and perhaps fraudulent religious leader Pontneuf attempts to manipulate Lucas' emotional and mental state. An horrific incarceration and an appearance before a kangaroo court are not the worst of Lucas' experiences as he searches for answers to explain his seeming betrayal by Nuria, the woman he thought he had fallen in love with.

The Colour of a Dog Running Away presents an engaging tableau of life at the end of the twentieth century in this magical city populated with nomads. The displaced characters that make up the tale are representatives of modern urban life, lonely and spiritually bereft and, like the events described in the novel, somewhat chaotic and unpredictable.

Richard Gwyn has clearly been influenced by postmodern fiction and its emphasis on the city and its ambiguous environmental space, and this is mirrored in the narrative's resistance to traditional closure and verisimilitude.

Arguably though, the real appeal of the writing is not in this self-conscious stylisation but in the author's evident love for Barcelona itself. His choice of a writer-translator as narrator, a literary broker between cultures and languages, is inspired. All in all, this is an entertaining and readable tale and tribute to the dazzling capital of Catalonia. SRR

)> I walked with Igbar back towards his flat, embraced him, and left him there, then continued up Carders, across Laietana, and over to the Ramblas. The evening was already drawing in. I must have spent longer with Igbar than I had thought. But I was in no hurry, settling instead into a kind of waiting game. Something, I was certain, was going to happen today. On the way down Ferran I bought a Havana cigar, and at the bottom of the street took a right and went to the Café de l'Opera on the Ramblas. Here was a place with a view, one that in the past had given me hours of pleasure, people-watching. There was a spare table in the front part of the café, so I sat and smoked and ordered a coffee and a brandy. The usual parade of dramatically weathered old queens, self-consciously artistic types, voluble Catalan theatre-goers, enthusiastic young Americans, and voyeurs (like myself) were attended in turn by the efficient and indifferent waiters. A parodic rendition of a vanished café society. **((** 334–5

Hughes, Tristan

The Tower

Place has been defined in one contemporary version as 'space to which meaning has been ascribed', and it is the meanings that we apply to land and space that Hughes considers in *The Tower*. The book is a collection of seven beautifully written and interwoven short stories that look at the same 'small patch of land' on Ynys Môn (the Isle of Anglesey). As well as exploring how this specific place influences — and indeed is influenced by — a cast of diverse characters,

Hughes also considers wider issues of place and the importance of the notions of 'here', 'somewhere' and 'nowhere'. Some characters seem stranded on the *ynys*, unsure of how they came to be there, while others come to realise how they have been left behind.

Each story offers a different perspective on the 'tower' of the book's title — an old windmill. Nain recalls when the windmill, now being renovated for Derrick Dallas's nouveau riche Liverpudlian friends, was working, and how the last miller ceased the sails. Derrick's own story reveals an unexpected profundity; a man who does not belong anywhere tries to create a vision of a place where he does belong, but is ultimately unable to perceive it. His builders, meanwhile, spend a weekend gathering magic mushrooms, drinking and wishing that they were somewhere other than Ynys Môn. Skinner and his unhappy girlfriend Gemma are two hippies stuck in a leaking caravan in Jac Cucu's field; Skinner believes that he can map the 'good/natural powers' of the island, while Gemma attempts to trace how she came to be so lost. Jac Cucu reveals how his name is not his own, but part of his inheritance, along with the land that he is bound to. The local vicar writes letters to his émigré brother in America, yet never sends them, and so becomes ever more grounded in a place he cannot leave. Finally, we hear Alun's story, a character who on returning to Môn realises that he has lost more than he had expected.

As well as exploring the poignant stories of those who live in the shadow of the tower, the book also investigates the space between the long natural history of the land and the relatively contemporary human history of the island. This is best illustrated in the story 'Of Rocks and Stones' by the juxtaposition of the fossils contained in the stones that make the monuments of community — in this case, Bethania Chapel — and the social history contained within the building. The importance of stones — and therefore the land — to social and cultural history is also refracted though the druidic standing stones of Jac Cucu's fields, and Skinner's defence of them and the mystic tradition of the island. Hughes also considers the space between the enduring and the transient, and especially our perception and negotiation of this space — how people strive to leave a legacy while also coping with the legacies they inherit and those they collect along the way. In its exploration of place and the meanings attributed to it, *The Tower* maps a common *hiraeth** for the actual and metaphoric places and spaces we sometimes cannot fully locate. SM

**hiraeth*: a feeling of longing or loss related to home and heritage and a pervading theme in Welsh literature

)) 'Listening to Jack she had thought how every story was really an elegy, how they were populated with dead people, and took place in ruined houses, and happened in dead times. Outside, the landscape was just a huge, patterned graveyard, each field a plot, each wall a gravestone, each cluster of trees a forgotten bouquet of flowers. She had thought about Skinner's map, and how maps were just a story about the ground beneath, an epitaph written in cold, mute lines. Jack had only asked her one question, her own question repeated: why was she here. And she knew that she didn't have an answer and she knew she didn't want to keep on not having one. And more than anything else she wanted to go home'. **((** 49

Humphreys, Emyr

Outside the House of Baal

A Man's Estate

Outside the House of Baal, a book from the mid-1960s, is considered one of the most canonical of modern Welsh novels. It tackles thorny problems of Welsh identity in the twentieth century and beyond, including the effects of the dissolution of the 'niche civilisation' of Welsh-speaking Nonconformism, seen for example in the dialogue between the book's main protagonist, philosophically troubled preacher J.T. Miles, and his son Ronnie who is, tellingly, a sociologist rather than a man of the cloth.

To his father's chagrin Ronnie speaks of a 'dead-wood' tradition while a new pub, the so-called (by J.T.) 'House of Baal' now abuts onto his garden. The preacher understands temperance as something firmly Welsh, in contradistinction to the easy ways the pub represents, and in this context also an encroaching Englishness. It is a good representation of the fatal collisions between ethnicity, religious orthodoxy and acculturation, experienced not only in Wales but right across the world. In *Outside the House of Baal* Humphreys tries to seek out and closely describe individual bearers of the Welsh Nonconformist culture, presenting in particular detailed word pictures of the preacher Miles and his sister Kate. Like R.S. Thomas he is a religiously-minded cherisher of his small nation and its people and writes with a sense of national crisis. The level of attention to both prosaic everyday detail (down to the 'she opened the drawer' type of events) and to the moral quandaries of what to most of us will seem like a distant age can make this seem rather a slow-running stream of a book, a super-extended *Bildungsroman*, following J.T. Miles through childhood and adolescence, theological studies and, perhaps over-ambitiously, right through middle and old age. In some ways this is more of a literary monument than a readable novel for today, packing together as it does documentary novel with crisis of belief essay and family saga. Still, monuments are often well worth a visit. . .

An important if less canonical work, *A Man's Estate*, was published ten years earlier in 1955 and is far more accessible, perhaps because less ambitious. Its main theme is however a related one; it deals with the Welshman and woman's connection to their historical landscape, a theme that increasing globalisation and cultural homogenisation makes as relevant as ever.

Humphreys' speciality is considered to be the echoing of these national concerns, widely posed in Welsh-language writing, through the medium of the realist English-language 'regional novel'. Early on, for example, we hear the young Philip Esmor-Elis, who has been physically and emotionally exiled from his native corner, say 'When I hear the word Welsh I feel uncomfortable'.

A Man's Estate is a story that combines traces of a modern (1950s) world of competing academics, luxury country hotels and 'motor garages' with the sexual misdeeds of the Edwardian age, flavoured by melodrama: swapped babies, a poisoning and a snaffled inheritance.

The cockpit of this struggle is the Elis family: 'We are the most important family in the district, but our time is running out. By being what we are, we constitute the greatest bulwark in this small corner of Wales against the forces of change'. We have to read the crisis and history of this family as a metaphor, to some degree, for the wider Nonconformist society. Humphreys also treats us to some pretty nasty family dynamics, especially those at the expense of the vulnerable unmarried daughter Hannah. Her pillars-of-the-chapel parents, like everyone else in the book, are in fact more or less moral monsters. Indeed Humphreys rathers exults in describing the imperfect beings that make up the world. All the characters in *A Man's Estate* are grievously flawed, flawed in ways that prevent them from achieving or giving happiness or any other practical, useful good in the marketplace of humanity.

Humphreys described himself as a creator of 'Protestant novels' but here perhaps has as much written an anti-Protestant text, criticising the idea of careful, strained self-perfection that this faith has at its centre, condemning it as being about conformity of outward appearance at the expense of inner charitableness or warmth. Perhaps that was his point.

A Man's Estate has a lively narrative structure of different narrators and viewpoints and is arguably more modern in form than the book that followed it ten years later. Another book by Humphreys, *A Toy Epic*, is reviewed in the Welsh-language section of this *Babel Guide*. RK

) J.T. smiled and scratched his head.

– In every respect, Griff said.

He fell silent, pulling at a long stem of grass as if he could say more and preferred not to.

– What do you mean?

J.T. leaned towards him to catch what he might murmur.

I don't believe any of it, Griff said.

He kept his gaze fixed steadily on J.T.'s face gauging the effect of his words.

Not one word, he said.

J.T. said nothing. The hum of the wild bees in the brambles on the edge of the quarry nearest to where they sat seemed to grow louder in the silence. At last J.T. cleared his throat.

– Do you mean, he said hoarsely, do you mean you've lost your faith?

– If that's the way you want to put it, Griff said. I just can't go on swallowing it all any more.

– Swallowing what? J.T. said.

Talking about God as if he were the Moderator of the Free Church Council, Griff said. As though our denomination owned him and kept him in a box under the pulpit and stood on it every Sunday. As if he went over the accounts of every chapel with the two other members of the Trinity and signed them with 'examined and found correct'.

Griff made a gesture with the stem of grass as if it were a pen and he was signing a document with a flourish.

I admit there is too much emphasis on organisation in our Connexion, J.T. said slowly. There is too much talk about collections and funds and. . .

– Listen, Griff said. I'm not arguing. I'm confessing. I don't believe a single word of any of it.

Outside the House of Baal 110

"'The young people of today have got no interest in music," said Parry Castle Stores. "Not a scrap. It's most disheartening."

"When I was a young man," Elis the Chemist said, "we had an excellent Young Temperance Society attached to Bethania. It did enormous good. It was militant. It got things done. Forced the public houses in the district to close on Sundays. We had processions. Do you intend to have processions, Mr Powell?"

"I hadn't thought of it, Mr Elis. But thank you for the suggestion."''

A Man's Estate **‹‹** 82–83

James, Siân

A Small Country

This is the story of a Welsh farming family in the process of dissolution, both sentimentally and socially, in the period just before World War One. While the setting is idyllic enough — 'it was a still, silvery morning, doves murmuring from the huge chestnut trees outside the windows' — this large house with its small staff of loyal retainers is struck with great unhappiness as the head of the family, Josi, runs off with a young(ish) female teacher he encounters by chance one day.

There are echoes of D.H. Lawrence's *Lady Chatterley's Lover* (a work whose importance has been traduced by its notoriety) in the foregrounding of sexual passion in the lives of the main protagonists and it is set in a similar period.

There are echoes too in the figure of the then recently-minted 'independent woman' and the related suffragette agitation that bears strongly on the lives of two of the book's female characters. The contrast with Lawrence, though, is that he celebrated sexual passion as the truth-tiger in a hypocritical and emotionally-stifled world while James, writing in the late 1970s, grievously punishes every single one of her characters who open themselves to their sexual feelings. This reader can't help feeling that the book was written along that tricky faultline where feminism and Protestant Puritanism met for tea and, finding things in common, formed an unholy alliance to trim the wings of 'libertinism'.

A more complex feminism is embedded in the character of Josi the wayward husband who is, strangely enough, although a wife-deserter a kind of male paragon in that his inner life is directed not by his own desires but by those of the women he encounters — he is if not a toyboy a 'toyman', first acquired by a richer older woman for a husband and then stolen by a fiery younger one for his looks and his obedience to her needs. While the book is perhaps partly opaque to itself in its standpoint James works with subtle, almost sly, characterisation to gain our involvement in the story she wants to tell us and adeptly outlines the emotional complexity and distributed hurt that results from a relationship triangle. RK

)) 'I have to get away, Edward, I must. I don't do my mother any good. It's only Tom and Nano she wants. It'll be worse than ever now that Father's left home; we'll live in a sort of mourning all our lives. I suppose I could escape by getting married, but I don't want to be a little black wife here in the country. You don't know what it's like, you've only been here on holiday. Nobody does anything interesting. Nobody seems to want to do anything but go to chapel and the weekly chapel meetings. The singing festival and the local eisteddfod are the

social highlights of the year. The ploughing contest is what we lose sleep over; they think I'm unnatural because I don't get excited about it. Our minister was publicly reprimanded because he took his seven-year-old son to the circus; it's the only thing I've ever respected him for, it's not that I approve of circuses but at least it's better than taking a child to a prayer meeting. But what is there for me to do? I'm not living, I'm existing. I've got to break out, I've got to, or I'll go mad.'
((50

Jenkins, Nigel

Gwalia in Khasia

The Khasia tribe live in an isolated part of north-east India, a mountainous land of virgin forests in the foothold of the Jaintia hills in Meghalay. On the one hand they form a progressive society in which women are treated with reverence, on the other the society is rather less enlightened in its practice of ritual sacrifice. The rich landscape is revered by its people who live in harmony with nature. Language is central too, revealing its proximity to the environment in its onomatopoeic emphasis: 'miaw' for cat and 'slap' for the heavy tropical rains that fall there. Their culture carries a weight of ancestral mythology and maintains its ancient oral tradition and this in fact is central to this beautifully crafted account of a meeting of two peoples bound by history and 'intervention'.

Combining both travelogue and historical account within a narrative structure, *Gwalia in Khasia* is the fascinating story of Wales' only overseas Mission, all but forgotten in the now quite secular homeland. Three distinct strands intertwine, Thomas Jones' mission, author Nigel Jenkins' adventure and the story of the Khasias themselves. Jenkins presents a complex portrait spanning two centuries and explores the ambiguous legacy of the venture for these mountain people.

The driving force of the narrative is a recreation of the mid-nineteenth century voyage when a young Thomas Jones leaves the poverty of his Welsh rural upbringing, obeying an evangelical call-to-arms. His determination to serve in India is irrepressible and he sets sail, with his pregnant wife, on 25 November 1840.

The trials faced by the embryonic mission: death, disease, extreme weather, rejection by the indigenous population and persecution by the colonial authorities are brought to life admirably. Jones is now revered by the Khasi people as the father of their literature, raising it as he did to the status of the written word. His contribution to Khasi life was both broad and far-reaching. A spiritual radical and pragmatist, Jones taught the people how to build their own homes and keep accounts and revolutionised the lime industry. This incurred the disapproval of his Church and the wrath of the corrupt colonialist bullyboy Harry Inglis, who brought about Jones' ultimate downfall.

Much of the narrative is given to the story of the tribe itself, particularly their incredible resilience in the face of cultural genocide — from British imperial subjugation, from missionary disregard for autochthonous culture, and more recently from a centralising Indian state.

Khasia today is a place of political turmoil, described first hand by Jenkins who, against the odds, procured a visa. He captures the Khasis in a precarious state, caught in the crossfire of history and he writes with a sensitivity of a Welshman implicated in their dilemma: simultaneously aware of his own country's struggle for identity and cultural autonomy.

This bleak history is leavened by the author's buoyant personality and the narrative is not without hope. His sense of humour is a refreshing counterpoint to this troubled region. With irreverent and delicious irony he mocks even his own undertaking, that this hidden history should be narrated by a 'hairy agnostic' 'with Buddhist leanings', whose own Welshness is in fact alien to the very tribesmen who continue to sing their own anthem to the tune of the Welsh national anthem, write their language using an alphabet based on Welsh orthography and who worship according to traditional Welsh Sunday custom.

Jenkins navigates this mythological, literary and political landscape with the same undisguised enthusiasm that characterises his vividly described meetings with the chapel-going, Kwai-chewing* locals. The surrounding landscape to which the tribe is fiercely attached is captured with lyricism and reverence. The reader gets the feeling that were it not for his domestic commitments in Wales, the narrator could quite happily set up camp among the Khasi to enjoy their poetry readings, beer infused camaraderie and ready hospitality. SRR

*Kwai is a combination of betel vine leaves, lime juice and betel nut

❱❱ 'My father was the Rev. E.B. Pugh, and I asked Daddy one day how we came by that name. He said his father must have taken it from some tombstone or other, presumably because he liked the sound of it'.

Khasis often do this kind of thing, and the consequences can be hilarious. People used to listen to missionaries or, in the last war, British soldiers, speaking English, and would get attracted to the sound of words without having a clue as to their meaning. So sometimes you get rather lovely names, like 'Milky Way' — or 'Whisky': sounds nice and tastes good. But then, again from the war, you run into dull names like 'Control Rate', or the string of boys called 'First Gear', 'Second Gear' and 'Third Gear'.

I remember the time a missionary was presented with a child at baptism, and when asked what he should christen the boy, was told 'Syphilis'. Not surprisingly, the missionary refused, and gave the child a name of his own choosing, but I believe the parents went on calling their boy 'Syphilis'. The same kind of problem arose with the parents who wanted to call their son 'Vagina'. **((** 126–7

Jones, Glyn

The Island of Apples

Glyn Jones, friend and contemporary of Dylan Thomas, was one of the most influential figures in the formative years of Welsh writing in English. *The Island of Apples*, perhaps his most important novel, is an elegy of youth and testament to a vanished community, the once vibrant industrial centre of Merthyr Tydfil. The fictional valley town of Ystrad functions as homage to the lively cultural and social milieu of the author's boyhood. In common with most English-language writers in Wales during this period, Jones explores the relationship between the industrial south and the rural west of his family origins.

Dewi Davies is a scholarship boy whose life is changed forever when a mysterious youth is saved from drowning by his father. Karl, the 'body' in the river, becomes the focus of adolescent hero-worship for the young protagonist, dazzled to the point of obsession by the exotic and charismatic older boy of undisclosed Central European origin. Karl provides an escape from the tragic realities of life — as Dewi experiences firstly the death of his father, in which Karl is implicated, and then his mother. Dewi's orphaned state, as seen through his own eyes, is barely touched upon, so great is his preoccupation with his idol. The rays of light that shine upon Karl's face in his last public confrontation with Growler, the school's headmaster, accentuate his role as saviour to the impressionable Dewi. Family bereavement provides an opportunity for Dewi to stay with his beloved friend though any semblance of stability and protection are shattered when Karl is incriminated in a serious arson charge and later becomes a prime murder suspect.

The novel's characters filter through a child's imagination. Grotesque Mr Powell, hideous authority figure Growler, formidable mother — always 'bossy and domineering' — 'furry' father and alcoholic uncle all figure in cameo because of Dewi's distinct obsession with Karl. But his faith in Karl is severely tested in the final part of the novel, even though he decides to follow him to the end. Seemingly immortal, Karl survives numerous near-death experiences and the novel ends ambiguously with his disappearance into the rapids, fittingly during a great storm, illustrating Jones' clear debt to the Romantic poets, with nature reflecting the inner life of the sensitive protagonist.

A novel of 'pre-adolescence', *The Island of Apples* is narrated in an entertainingly naïve and exaggerated register. As young Dewi grows up to face the darker side of life, Jones effectively captures both a child's psychology and the rites of passage into manhood. The immature mind, conflating fantasy with reality, is well caught too in the idealised Karl, with Dewi's feelings of adoration and wonder delineated in first-person prose.

The novel's real strength, though, lies in its portrayal of Dewi coming to terms with tragedy and loss, in witnessing the death of his parents, seeing the bodies of Powell and later Growler, but most of all, in the impact on his boyhood imagination of Karl's downfall. The 'Island of Apples' or *Ynys Afallon*, the ancient Celtic land of eternal youth and abundant joy, is a fitting title for this intense, sensual narrative showing the considerable vitality of a particular place, Merthyr Tydfil, at a particular moment. First published back in 1965, the book maintains its status as a fine classic of adolescent wish-fulfilment. SRR

)) Every Saturday, as soon as I got back from my granny's, Karl and I went off together, it was marvellous. Sometimes Jeffy, Tom and Charley came with us, or one or two of them, but usually we went by ourselves because we could stay out as long as we wanted to, not like them, and there was nobody to badger us about where we'd been, and who was with us, and what we'd had to eat, and when, and that. We went out at night as well, sometimes, when we were supposed to be in bed, and Karl used to mesmerize me before we went down the timber balks, because whenever I had to climb anywhere my head began to buzz as though a few thousand bees were among the blossoms inside there, and it got so swimmy I couldn't move. But after Karl had passed his hands in front of my face a few times, and muttered some special incantations he had, I always felt brave, I would have gone goating up the Nannies after him then if he'd told me to. **((** 182–3

Jones, John Sam

Welsh Boys Too!

In 1924 E.Prosser Rhys won the crown at the National Eisteddfod for his hugely controversial ode *Atgof* ('Memory') which dealt with the sexual awakening of a young gay man. It scandalised this invariably conservative institution and though John Sam Jones writes in English, his stories are set in the Welsh-language heartland formed by the same religious Nonconformity and cultural politics depicted by Rhys seventy years ago.

John Sam Jones' prize-winning first collection was inspired by his own experiences as a gay youth in the traditionally Welsh-speaking rural hinterland of a small coastal town.

Jones is often preoccupied with the individual's sense of belonging and the need to negotiate a place in his community. The shifts in narrative perspectives, for example in 'Sharks on the Bedroom Floor', emphasise that selfhood is not fixed or definitive but exists in relationship to different factors. By challenging narrow notions of identity, Jones is attempting to undermine the prejudice that maintains 'traditional values'. In fact, from his first story that recounts a holiday hiking in the Polish mountains, intolerance, here in the extreme case of Auschwitz and the Holocaust, is a central theme.

To expose bigotry in his own community Jones employs several narrative voices, with each story dedicated to a central male character. He presents negative stereotypes as well as refreshing counter-images that undermine them. The characters and situations portrayed in *Welsh Boys Too!* range from the first flush of attraction between Gethin and Berndt in 'The Wonder at Seal Cave', to the outrageously promiscuous Mark in 'Etienne's Vineyard' as well as describing the domestic routine of Rhodri and Justin in 'Sharks on the Bedroom Floor'. Perhaps the most poignant aspect of the collection is the concern for young men coming to terms with their sexuality in a rejecting society that frequently imposes depression, confusion and self-loathing on them.

In 'But names will never hurt me' Arfon has been bullied and abused. He's depressed and driven to a series of destructive encounters. Seventeen years old, like the middle-class Gethin in 'The Wonder at Seal Cave', he can find no role-models in his community. Even when explicitly sought no guidance is given; these are young men systematically let down by school and family. Sam Rees in 'My Velvet Eyes' bears the scars of such rejection — 'a gay son is as good as a dead son'. He is disowned by his father and excluded from his mother's funeral. He then rejects any vestiges of his past: his family, his language and his culture are all buried along with the mother he has not been allowed to mourn.

Other stories also illustrate explicit homophobia in Wales, as in the attitude of the Reverend Llŷr Jones who believes that homosexuals are 'disturbed and [in need of] psychiatric treatment'. Sometimes less explicit but equally insidious prejudice crops up as, for example, the hilarious exchange with the salesperson at the Asleep-eezy shop in the concluding story. But not all responses are negative and rejecting — there is love and acceptance from Rhodri's niece and nephew in 'Sharks on the Bedroom Floor' and the compassion and care of Glyn's aunt in the 'Magenta Silk Thread'.

Jones' prose is unpretentious, direct, without hyperbole; the reader is presented with the reality of being a gay man in small-town Wales. While revealing the harsh facts of social ostracism, family denial, rejection and prejudice Jones tempers his work with a lightness of touch and genuine humour. SRR

)) Once they'd declared their interest in the lower end of the up-market ranges the assistant at Asleep-eezy followed them around like a sissy's poodle.

'We'd like to take a look on our own if that's all right,' Tom said, echoing her tone of forced politeness. 'We'll come to you if we've got any questions'.

'Oh. It's no trouble, gentlemen. I'm Mrs Chessington, the senior floor manager,' she said obsequiously. 'I'm here to make sure that you know exactly what kind of bed it is you want, and more importantly, to help you know what you're getting for your money once you've decided. Good beds don't come cheap, gentlemen. Now then,' she said, upping her tone into the bossy range, 'it's a single you're looking for, is it?' **((** 'Pocket Sprung and Nested' 86–7

Jones, Lloyd

Mr Vogel

This novel in three distinct sections — the symbolism of which only becomes clear at the end — is itself, as the author describes the land of Wales, a bag of tricks. Once opened it fascinates with its rush of styles, characters, temporal shifts and mythical proportions. A book with a dark secret but ultimately hopeful in spirit, in it we make a breathtaking journey that begins with the discovery of a manuscript.

With a flourish, we are thrust into an anachronistic fairytale world set in and around the infamous Blue Angel pub with narration supplied by its quirky bartender. A motley crew of characters frequent the place, including explorers like George Borrow and Thomas Pennant. Humboldt's parrot is also in residence and a Welsh Don Quixote drops by regularly. The narrative explodes outwards to eventually encapsulate Welsh history in a cleverly exploited world of make-believe, set in a handy time-warp that allows past and present to converge.

This is the 'second home' of Mr Vogel — a solitary physically disabled man whose life is changed when he wins a competition. The tone of the 'Vogel Papers' blends comic grandeur and allegory with children's fantasy and a Mabinogion-like* quest narrative. Vogel is the archetypal anti-hero, planning an improbable mission to realise his dream.

Part Two of the book goes on to give a voice to the discoverer of the manuscript, an apparently objective narrator who, as an adjunct to his fascination with the lame protagonist, decides to undergo a 'middle-aged rite of passage' himself. His quest is to walk the whole of Wales as a roving detective in search of Vogel. He makes the entire country his playground, examining its fabric with a fervid curiosity.

The trek around the nation allows the walker his own flight of fancy that neatly mirrors Vogel's own. A prig at times, he shares many characteristics with Vogel such as his frugality and his friends, 'Waldo' and 'Paddy', are clearly the Don and Sancho Panza of Part One. The narrative voice, like Vogel's, is by turns colloquial and erudite. Events, characters and themes are replayed but the urgency of solving Vogel's mystery maintains a certain narrative realism throughout.

Vogel, frail and broken, emerges from the fragments of this created past in the final section of the novel. Gwydion, the quintessential storyteller of Welsh mythology, here a bookshop-owner and temporary fellow patient with Vogel in a psychiatric unit, is charged with the task of meaning-making. This pantomime of origins, shrouded in fantasy, becomes a commissioned chronicle of identity, enacted in a ward for the mentally ill: 'Tell them how I feel inside, not how I look or act,' pleads Vogel. Gradually the subtext is revealed: Vogel is an alcoholic.

This allusive and symbolic novel draws attention to its text as an artificial construct and this emphasises a central theme: the relationship between our fantasies or fictions and our reality. At the same time the collective consciousness of a small nation is somehow captured in Vogel's adventure while, in its labyrinthine and fantastical way, it comically and sometimes movingly portrays a triumph over terrible obstacles and the achievement of personal salvation. SRR

*A collection of medieval Welsh prose tales

)) I sat atop Hay Bluff and fermented with happiness. The only human near me was a shepherd on horseback way below me, whistling to his dogs, and funnelling his sheep towards a gate into an upland field; they massed there like fat platelets around a newly-opened wound, then disappeared slowly and left me gloriously alone.

I met a woman once who said that mountain people are up and down, people of the plains are temperamentally flat. Seems like a flat earth theory, but these old ideas, handed down over generations, often have a nub of truth. I was born on the side of a hill, and sure enough, I'm up and down like a paternoster lift.

Midlanders are well-known for being unflappable and unexcitable. Could be something in it.

Me, I get silly happy on mountains. **((** 134

Jones, Russell Celyn

Soldiers and Innocents

During the mid-1980s, a soldier of an elite airborne regiment goes absent without leave from active service in Northern Ireland after witnessing the death of a woman in labour, and the subsequent suicide of her mother. The stillborn child, whose image concludes the novel's prologue, is the catalyst that forces Captain Evan Price to question the morality of the army and the state that governs it. He can no longer accept the conditioning imposed by military training that strips men of their personal and communal responsibilities. It is this realisation that compels him to return to his roots and take greater responsibility as the father of a young son.

The novel follows the journey of a young man driven to comprehend his place in the world. The army denies him autonomy and presents itself as an all-encompassing family, a completely self-contained community. Evan comes to view these bonds as essentially malevolent, based on violence and subjugation without regard for the sanctity of life, 'a system that generated evil as a way of sustaining itself'.

The guiding factor for Evan's actions following his desertion is his renewed commitment to fatherhood. This one time 'mystery in jungle green' or 'part-time' presence, as his estranged wife refers to him, feels a desperate need to bond with his son, five-year-old Terence. Having been formed by a career based on blind courage and fearlessness, Evan now finds himself at his most vulnerable and uncertain as he struggles to be a parent to a boy he barely knows: 'Evan told himself that he was not a cruel father, only an inadequate one, unprepared. In his world, all men are amateur parents, if they are lucky enough to get to play parent at all. In Evan's world the men went to war while the women raised the children single-handed'.

The reader becomes aware that Terence has been taken from school by his father, without the consent of his mother, as a desperate act of atonement. Evan's awkward, unauthorised, and inappropriate parenting invokes memories of his own childhood and the strained relationship he had with his father.

Retreating after a decade's absence to the once-bustling Welsh valley town of his youth, Evan is shocked by the decay in what is now essentially a 'dead' town. He compares this desolation with Belfast and sees the same legacy of a 'colonizing culture'. The army exists to preserve this inequality and Evan, up until now, has colluded unremittingly. In the old family home in Craig Street, Evan is forced to confront the troubling elements in his own past and to take responsibility for his actions, and their consequences, in the present.

His father's experiences as a soldier in the same battalion in World War Two provide a striking contrast to active service in Northern Ireland. According to Evan 'the only reason British troops are in Ireland today is to keep them bloodied'. He is angry about the British Army's role in the Ulster conflict and sees it as a training exercise for future conflicts. His father is of a different generation and mindset. His loyalty to his regiment 2 Para is unflinching. The old man cannot forgive his son for the 'shame' he has brought upon the family and cannot comprehend the motivations for his behaviour.

Evan is heir to these essentially patriarchal values within a community where 'miners make good soldiers'. His father had pushed Evan towards boxing, wishing him to be a prizefighter, unable to accept his son's inevitable failure. Evan bends to his father's will, joining the army and accepting a culture of machismo where 'there was nothing a man could do to shake it off'. Nine and a half years later, father and son still cannot talk to each other and Evan is not able to forgive.

The father dies. There is no reconciliation. But the return signals a new realisation for Evan. He is reunited with his sisters and this female intervention, specifically from his older sister Beth, nurtures a new awareness of family ties, free from the negative conditioning imposed by his father and army dogma.

The army, epitomised by Evan's father, has failed to respond to a changing human landscape. '. . . society evolves but its army remains a static metaphor of manhood in its most rigid and malevolent form. Soldiers are dinosaurs'. Evan re-evaluates his life, galvanized by his encounters with 'innocents' — the tragic deaths he witnesses in Northern Ireland, his downtrodden mother, his estranged wife and, most significantly, his vulnerable young son. He rejects a seemingly sterile version of masculinity.

The overall starkness of *Soldiers and Innocents* captures the guilt, nihilism and tension that have fuelled Evan's existence. The sharp order of conditioned routine is well evoked in a tight narrative. Evan's experiences with his father and his developing relationship with his own little boy allow him in the end to discover regenerative aspects of human relationships outside the harsh world of the military. SRR

)) 'Are you still a soldier?'

'Not at the moment'.

'Then why have you got a gun? Soldiers have got guns'.

'Military instincts, Terence. A little harder to shed than a uniform. Come outside with me and I'll show you how to use it'.

'I'm hungry'.

'So let's go and shoot breakfast'.

'You said you'd buy me a cake from the shop'.

'Well, yes. But the shop was closed, old man,' Evan lied. He had forgotten all about the cake, was a bad victualler. **((** 105

Knight, Stephen

Mr Schnitzel

Winner of the Arts Council of Wales 'Book of the Year Award' in 2001, *Mr Schnitzel* evades categorisation: it's a novel, a book of fables, a memoir, even a travelogue. Despite this ambiguous and sometimes fragmentary format, it has an impressive coherence and gravitas.

Night after night, while Stefan and his family are visiting his mother's aunt in Austria, his father (the eponymous Mr Schnitzel — 'an honorary title' bestowed on account of his fondness for that particular dish) tells him fairytales about the Austrian Navy: 'Stories for a five-year-old unsettled by sleeping in a strange bed in a strange country'. Among the characters Stefan is introduced to are Elfrieda the heartbroken pirate, bent on revenging her husband's murder; compulsive potholer Thomas von Gammon and his doomed exploration of Europe's subterranean canals; and Count Otto von Otto, First Admiral of the Austrian Fleet and 'an excellent swimmer', dispatched to scupper the Turkish Armada using the pickelhaube, or spike, on the top of his helmet.

Accompanying these fantastic tales are autobiographical digressions in the form of footnotes, which sometimes come to occupy all but a few lines of a page. They tell another, apparently truer, story: that of a middle-class family from a vividly-evoked suburban 1970s south Wales, and of Stefan's mother's life, her self-imposed exile from the land of her birth, and the grief, guilt and ultimate mental collapse that gives rise to.

The book is scattered with charming but often gritty accounts of Stefan's childhood and adolescence, his kind but timorous father, and his parents' painful marriage, as well as the family holidays to Austria and the relatives his mother left behind there as a young woman.

Although *Mr Schnitzel*'s most famous literary antecedent is probably Nabokov's *Pale Fire* (where a long annotated poem precedes a fictional 'commentary'), it also brings to mind the serious playfulness of European writers like Calvino and Perec, as well as some recent Welsh novels in which fact and fiction, fable and biography, are allowed to merge such as Owen Sheers' novel/travelogue/biography, *The Dust Diaries* or Lloyd Jones' Welsh picaresque, *Mr Vogel*.

Stephen Knight is also the author of two poetry collections and the writing here is often poetic, with a nonchalant facility for imagery (a sink 'girdled with dirt'; carpets fraying at the edges, 'like Dougal from The Magic Roundabout'). True, Mr Schnitzel's form makes uncommon demands of the reader, by disrupting the traditionally linear activity of reading — just as a fable gets going, a footnote draws your attention to an autobiographical sketch which often goes on for five or six pages while the fable continues 'overhead', obliging you to flick back to resume the fable once the footnote finishes — but somehow this never becomes tiresome.

The text is laid out with considerable skill and although the footnotes appear to be scattered rather arbitrarily, form and subject-matter seem ideally wed. As we grow familiar with the intertwining worlds of 'fact' and 'fantasy' here it becomes clear how strongly they inform and illuminate one another. At its heart, Schnitzel is a reflection on the roots of story, on the consolations of an author's work and the alchemy by which life becomes art. WA

)> In the dying days of the nineteenth century, Ute, the youngest daughter of Wilhelm, Admiral of the Fleet, became a prisoner of her father's twin obsessions, ships and the fear that his favourite girl might one day be spirited away by a wholly inappropriate suitor. Wilhelm dreaded his baby meeting a man who didn't have a steady income, a man who couldn't erect a shelf, a deadbeat, or, worst of all, a German. He settled on a way to combine these two obsessions when the burghers of Maria Wörth offered to pay for the construction of any monument he desired, a gesture of gratitude for one of his great maritime victories against the Swedes… 9

Their plaster smooth as skin, the buildings of Maria Wörth are dazzlingly white and the lake is as clear as air — its pin-sharp reeds, pebbles and trout (placid amnesiacs nudging one another) must have been out of our depth, though it seemed as if we could have knelt on the bridge to dip our hands in the water and touch them… 61 **((**

Lewis, Gwyneth

Two in a Boat: A Marital Voyage

Gwyneth Lewis is an acclaimed poet, one of the twenty listed in the 2004 New Generation Poets*. She is arguably Wales' best bilingual poet, author of one of the biggest poems in the world**, the enormous symbol of Wales' new cultural and political autonomy in Cardiff Bay's docklands. Like all good poets she seeks out new territories of the mind exploring, like her astronaut cousin***, new worlds and means of navigation. *Two in a Boat* is Lewis' lyrical prose account of a life-changing venture on a beautiful old 'Nicholson 35' yacht, the *Jameelah*.

Hooked on C.S. Forester's 'Hornblower' books (historical novels about the British Royal Navy) and inspired by her own father's seafaring past, a tarot reading by a chain-smoking neighbour sows the final seeds as Lewis, and her ex-bosun husband Leighton, renounce their landlubber existence for a life on the open seas. Lewis seeks the calm and strength required of a sailor to balance her years of debilitating depression and alcoholism. The journey becomes a galvanising force that will enable her to 'break out of the compulsive maps of old behaviour that had led to shipwreck time and again'.

And so an innumerate poet, who suffers terrible seasickness, and her dyslexic pensioner husband embark on a journey that will test their physical and emotional endurance to the limit. The reader is given an insight into the practical preparations, the complexities and dangers involved but at no point does the narrative become overladen with technical jargon. Lewis is always entertaining and her enthusiasm for the subject means that the reader is drawn into the false starts, siren distractions and time-consuming logistical problems. Sometimes the prose has a startling and breathless quality, for example, the encounter on the perilous Breton coast with fog, trawlers and pitch-black night.

The book is also a homage to seafaring through the centuries, from the Phoenicians and early Celts through Portuguese discoverers and Lord Nelson up to the astonishing Ellen MacArthur**** whom the couple meet during their own voyage. Lewis also follows the extraordinary journey of Welsh coal — once the essential fuel of Empire — around the globe. Cardiff, where she grew up and one of the biggest industrial ports in the world in its heyday, is a constant reference point on her map of the high seas.

But the real narrative dynamic here is that between husband and wife. The boat, and all its paraphernalia, becomes a metaphor for that relationship and their marriage is opened up by the heightened awareness and clarity the confines of *Jameelah* and the journey itself provide. Leighton is her rock on land — a role he fulfils with compassion and selflessness, but at sea he becomes the one-dimensional 'Captain Bastard'.

Lewis both examines her past and imagines the potential changes this new experience will deliver for the future. This provides a new belief only overshadowed by feelings of helplessness and despair at the 'old' Leighton's disappearance. Their relationship becomes more turbulent as continual problems with the engine, exacerbated by unscrupulous mechanics, threaten to end their journey prematurely. Finally however, it is a more menacing and insidious force that defeats their dreams. Leighton, who changed so dramatically (and now understandably) during the course of their voyage, is diagnosed with cancer.

Two in a Boat gives the reader a privileged insight into a very intimate relationship, painstakingly observed. It cleverly intertwines the practicalities of life at sea (throughout history) with fantasies of exotic locations and idealised seafarers. The destination is less important than the process of learning required to reach it, and for Lewis this means acceptance of all that has gone before: 'I've always had a hunch that travelling is less a matter of seeking out new experiences than of moving towards your own past'. SRR

*The 20 'New Generation' UK poets were selected on the basis of a first single author collection published between 1994 and 2004

**written on the whole of one side of a new building, the Wales Millenium Centre, that now dominates the Cardiff bay skyline

***Joe Tanner, an astronaut who worked on the Hubble telescope in 1997. Lewis wrote her collection *Zero Gravity* with this as its background

****British yachtswoman who, at 24, sailed around the world in 94 days

)) Neither of us said anything but we were both thinking the same things. We had spent all that money and still didn't have a working engine; those months of discomfort in Leixōs had been for nothing; the boat was breaking us both; we had been fools to think we could make such a voyage.

Then, suddenly, in the middle of it all, the night became astonishingly beautiful. I was beginning to understand the Zen of the boat. You do something that's difficult, that shows up all your awkwardness and helplessness and then, because there's nowhere to go except onwards, no one to blame while you're out at sea, you start surprising yourself. After you've wept with rage and frustration and vowed never to leave land again, things start unfolding and showing themselves to you.

My despair flipped into exultation. Here we were, sailing through black velvet water, with phosphorescence in our wake. ((188

Meredith, Christopher

Griffri

One of the characters in Christopher Meredith's debut novel, *Shifts* (1988), was an amateur historian whose investigations into the industrial origins of his Valleys town lead him towards a partial reclamation of a Welsh-language culture and identity lost to the present. Meredith's second full-length fiction, *Griffri* (1991), might similarly be seen as an attempt to reclaim the Welshness of this same south-eastern corner of Wales, taking the reader back to a period, the twelfth century, when the region (Meredith's own) stood at the vanguard of Welsh resistance to Anglo-Norman invaders. In a vivid first-person narrative, this powerfully imagined and meticulously researched novel tells the life story of Griffri ap Berddig, *pencerdd* or 'chief poet' of the minor Welsh principality of Gwynllwg. Historically convincing yet also recognisably 'postmodern' in its concerns, *Griffri*'s narrative meditates on the relationship between choice and compulsion, truth and memory, knowledge and identity in language that is by turns gritty and lyrical, charting the brutal social, political and cultural impact of Norman colonisation.

This is not a straightforward historical novel. By avoiding the inclusion of maps and dates, and persistently questioning the reliability of narrative itself, Meredith foregrounds issues (particularly those relating to language and identity) central to contemporary cultural debates in Wales. In the process he treats the Welsh past not as an escape route to sidestep the uncomfortable realities of an anglicised present but rather to establish a critical relationship with this present. Significantly, Meredith portrays Wales' medieval past as a period, like the present, of flux, instability, and continual cultural exchange, thereby implying that there never was a time when Welsh culture and identity could be considered to have been 'pure'. In *Griffri*'s subtle depiction of the gradual adoption of Norman values, customs and codes of behaviour by the Welsh *uchelwyr* (noblemen), a sense of crisis and cultural fracture is suggestively conveyed, encouraging the reader to draw modern-day parallels. In claiming back the Welshness of Wales' south-eastern valleys, it is ironic that *Griffri* locates hybridity, and a concomitant sense of cultural erosion and crisis, at the very heart of what it means to be Welsh.

Griffi is undoubtedly a stimulating and thought-provoking novel albeit not one that, particularly for the non-Welsh reader, is always easy to read. Meredith makes few compromises in his depiction of historical and cultural otherness, and some readers may find the number of Welsh place and personal names in the text off-putting (although a limited glossary is provided, this is far from complete). Likewise, *Griffri*'s first-person narrative provides little in the way of historical context, and the reader without this knowledge is required to search for it elsewhere if they wish to appreciate fully all the nuances of Meredith's text. It is precisely this refusal to compromise, however, that might be regarded as *Griffri*'s great strength. In presenting this fictional account of a Welsh medieval life, Meredith refuses to erase the cultural gulf that lies between Griffri and ourselves. Nevertheless, without ever eliding the vast differences (social, cultural and political) between Wales past and Wales present, Meredith creates for the reader willing to make the effort a space in which the older Wales can be heard to speak, and speak rewardingly, even across the gulf of centuries. HR

)) I'd given Hywel the mail shirt I'd taken from my prisoner and he was wearing it now, though clearly it was heavy and uncomfortable. He carried his helmet with a finger hooked round the noseguard and there was a red mark on his forehead where it had sat.

'The helmet's set a mark on him', Meilyr said. He looked back to me. 'The escaping tower. Yes. It will fall without much pushing. Put out the lamps and they'll come round. Won't that be nice? And Iorwerth and Hywel can stride into their enlarged and Frenchified birthright wearing mail shirts and helmets. Won't that be glorious? We can cram it with our own acolytes. You and me, Griff, in the chancel, at the high altar of their shit cathedral. My friends'll love it there, crawling over Dyfrig's knucklebone. They'll enjoy the equation of sacrament and excrement'.

He laughed at his own cleverness, rubbed a hand on his crown. Then he peered at my shoulder. It was beginning to be dark and our fire was lighting us from below. He extended a hand, rubbed my shoulder, then sniffed his finger. I remembered the place where I'd leant against the wall of the fort, shaking and gasping before dawn. He laughed again.

'Now we're there', he said. 'Now we know ourselves'. **((** 196

Morris, Jan

Trieste and the Meaning of Nowhere

The author of more than forty books, including studies of Venice, Oxford, Manhattan, Sydney and Hong Kong, Jan Morris states in her Prologue to *Trieste and the Meaning of Nowhere* that this is to be her last publication. Fitting, then, that this portrait of a city which has 'curiously haunted' her since she first visited it as a soldier at the end of World War Two (an explanatory note tells readers that the author 'completed a change of sexual role in 1972'), should also be, in many ways, her most personal book. It is as much a reflection on the search for her own identity as on Trieste itself. 'For years,' she writes, 'I felt myself an exile from normality'. The book is also, to a large extent, a reiteration of themes — nationalism, empire and indeed exile — which have preoccupied Morris since her first book was published in 1956.

'The average traveller,' according to *Cook's Handbook* of 1925, 'would not make a point of staying long in Trieste'. As Morris herself admits, 'There are places that have meant more to me. . . My heart is in Wales'. The book is threaded with references to the author's Welsh homeland. She writes particularly poignantly of the islet on the river Dwyfor where her ashes will one day be scattered. The melancholy which, for Morris, characterises Trieste reminds her of the Welsh *hiraeth*, a malady to which the author is, one gathers, especially susceptible, and which she translates as 'an unspecified yearning'.

Trieste and the Meaning of Nowhere is both a celebration of an unusual and little-known city, and an exceptionally subtle meditation on the ageing process. Morris's presence in Trieste is wraithlike: she revisits herself as a gauche young soldier, sitting on the quayside trying to make sense of the world in his jotter. And Morris is an equally affable guide to historic Trieste, dropping in on the city in its imperial heyday and mingling unseen with the bourgeoisie, as well as the many writers who at one time or another made the city their home: Thomas Mann, Stendhal, Italo Svevo, Umberto Saba, and, most notably, James Joyce. The book is peppered with fictional flights of fancy, as when we are encouraged to eavesdrop on a grand reception at the house of the nineteenth-century tycoon Baron Revoltella: 'Up its velvet-railed staircase... we imagine the beau monde of Trieste sweeping with their fans and sashes, some genuinely flattered to be invited to the house of the legendary nabob, some still loftily condescending'. Pretension is wryly mocked and pomposity gently lanced, but like the 'citizens of nowhere' with whom she allies the people of Trieste, Morris 'suffers fools, if not gladly, at least sympathetically'.

One of the charms of this unconventional, intricate travelogue is its cast of characters, living and dead — the German art historian murdered in the Piazza Grande in 1768; the mad woman who verbally abuses the author before smiling sweetly and handing her the jumper she has dropped; 'Napoleon's youngest and raciest brother', Prince Jérôme; composer Baron Banfield-Tripcovich, 'a very gentlemanly man'; the 'spectacularly alarming' scholar and diplomat Sir Richard Burton — each drawn with warmth, humour, and a knack for the telling detail.

Travel, for Morris, is a series of encounters, with strangers, friends, and hitherto unknown facets of oneself. The book includes erudite and moving chapters on the Nazi liquidation of Trieste's Jews, on love, on kindness and civility, and concludes with a particularly memorable demolition of what Morris calls 'the nonsense of nationality,' in which she translates a definition of patriotism from the Welsh author and language activist, Saunders Lewis 'A generous spirit of love for civilisation and tradition and the best things of mankind'. Reading *Trieste and the Meaning of Nowhere*, one suspects that Lewis would have approved of Jan Morris' particular brand of patriotism. WA

❱❱ There are people everywhere who form a Fourth World, or a diaspora of their own. They are the lordly ones. They come in all colours. They can be Christians or Hindus or Muslims or Jews or pagans or atheists. They can be young or old, men or women, soldiers or pacifists, rich or poor. They may be patriots but they are never chauvinists. They share with each other, across all the nations, common values of humour and understanding. When you are among them you know you will not be mocked or resented, because they will not care about your race, your faith, your sex or your nationality, and they suffer fools if not gladly, at least sympathetically. They laugh easily. They are easily grateful. They are never mean. They are not inhibited by fashion, public opinion or political correctness. They are exiles in their own communities, because they are always in a minority, but they form a mighty nation, if only they knew it. It is the nation of nowhere, and I have come of think that its natural capital is Trieste. **((** 179

Rubens, Bernice

Brothers

My maternal grandfather, like one of Bernice Rubens' grandfathers, grew up in the Tsar's Russia and passed on three things from his life there: a gleaming brass samovar — the *sine qua non* of Russic domestic pride; my mother's frankly rather broken Yiddish, faint echo of a thousand years of Jewish Europe and one single, short but deafening item from the word-horde of the mighty Russian language: *pogrom*.

If anyone doesn't quite know what a pogrom was, then see Rubens' evocation here — description would be too bland a term — on pages 111 to 123.

Beyond this key set piece written with the passion and anger at the core of Rubens' work, *Brothers* documents Jewish life in the Russia from which the grandparents and great-grandparents of most of Britain's Jewish population escaped. As well as detailing the government-inspired pogroms we learn of other schemes of the various Tsars intent on destroying, dissolving or deporting the Jewish ethnic group they had unwillingly absorbed through territorial annexations of Poland. There was the special twenty-five years military service foisted on a large proportion of young Jewish males and the overnight decree contracting the area where Jews were permitted to reside, which deprived many of their homes and livelihoods from one day to the next.

It was this difficult and cruel situation as much as the search for better opportunities that led millions of Jews to emigrate to Western Europe and the New World, which is where Wales comes in because *Brothers* is a careful study of immigration as both a practical process and in its subtle psychological, cultural and emotional effects. A branch of the Russian-Jewish Bindel family at the heart of the book ends up in the Wales where Rubens herself grew up.

In this south Wales valleys setting she explores the drama of intermarriage and of the willed acculturation of all but the most religious Jews in emigration; 'in front of the children only English was spoken' — indicating the desire to leave behind 'Old Country' Jewishness and the cultural baggage of the Yiddish language in which its stories, humour and folk-knowledge were largely embedded.

With another part of the Bindel clan settling in Germany Rubens circles around that other major fact of the Jewish twentieth century, the Holocaust, in suitably angry and tragic pages but she also tells us the less-known but fascinating story of dissident Jews in later Soviet times when, to merely express the desire to emigrate to Israel or the West was 'an enemy act' punished, in the sober traditions of the Russian state, with loss of livelihood, false imprisonment and torture.

Alongside Rubens' passionate odium for what she saw as a largely unrepentant and unpunished Germany is her disdain, cleverly expressed in her characterisation of Russian officialdom both pre and post Soviet, for the steel-bound self-serving logic of all those who serve unjust authority, usually comfortably rewarded with privilege for their inhumanity.

Brothers is a genre masterpiece, that's to say while earthbound by the rather pat drama of its narrative unfolding, it yet manages to choose and treat its material cleverly and is frequently moving. At the end of a long career as a writer Rubens embraced *Brothers* as her best work, and it deserves to be read for its vision of Jewish destiny but also for its warm account of the working-class Welsh valleys people. Given the terrible fate of most European Jews within and without Russia, Rubens talks about Wales with the special feeling of gratitude felt by most British Jews, to these lands which, amongst their other virtues, granted refuge and livelihood to her and her parents. More about the Jewish-Welsh equation can be found in an excellent and unusually varied anthology of prose, essays and poetry *The Chosen People: Wales and the Jews*, edited by Grahame Davies in 2002. RK

» Night fell once more. Neither David nor Benjamin could sleep, but they linked arms and rocked against each other with the motion of the train.

'What are you thinking of, brother?' Benjamin asked.

'I have the same thoughts as you,' David said. 'We are both thinking of our children'.

In the morning the stench in the car was piteously severe, the odours of human waste now mixed with the smell of vomit. In time, Benjamin thought, the corpse at the end of the car would decompose. He wondered if one could ever get used to the smell of that. In the late afternoon, they heard the Kadish again, distant now, and doubly-spoken, for somewhere in the rear of the car, two human beings had been delivered.

'I wish you long life,' Leon said.

Another night passed, and in the morning, waking to the stench, they wondered how long they could still be alive, and they marvelled at human endurance, and began for the first time to have faith in their survival. Then suddenly the train stopped and did not start again.

'We shall have air,' someone cried. 'God is good,' and the crowd echoed his thanksgiving. That's all they wanted from life. Not food, not water. Just air. And suddenly the doors slid open.

They were blinded by the light, and intoxicated by the astonished air. Some fainted where they stood, and some were trampled on by those in a frantic rush for escape from the car. The Bindel family were among the first to alight from the wagon, and they breathed deeply of the biting and cold air. Benjamin waited at the doors helping the passengers alight, and waiting for the mother whom he had delivered and a new sight of his namesake. She came to the front of the wagon and handed him the baby. Then her husband jumped to the ground and lifted her down. 'Where are we?' she said, as she gulped for air.

Benjamin looked at his surroundings for the first time. They were bleak and reminded him fearfully of Buchenwald. For this was a camp too, though on a vaster scale, its perimeters beyond the eyes' reach, and despite the noise and cries of the new arrivals, as silent as the grave. Some storm-troopers leapt onto the wagon and hurried the remaining passengers outside, beating them with their sticks if they were tardy. 'Where are we?' a woman screamed, her eyes blinded by the light. 'Auschwitz,' a guard said, and that was the first time that many of the arrivals had heard the word, a simple German bi-syllable. A place and a name. **⟪** 352

Sheers, Owen

The Dust Diaries

The Dust Diaries is the ambitious and accomplished first novel of poet Owen Sheers. It is a multi-faceted work on the life of the Reverend Arthur Shearly Cripps — at once a novel, a biography, a memoir, a travelogue, an account of social history, war and imperialism and a love story. Sheers describes *Dust Diaries* as 'the story of Arthur Cripps' life reflected through my imagination' but it is based on extensive research into the life and surroundings of this socially aware missionary to the Shona people of Zimbabwe.

The book is constructed from intricately layered narratives — the novel spans the twentieth century as author Owen Sheers' experiences of contemporary Zimbabwe are interspersed with accounts of Cripps' last days, memories of his time in Africa as well as of the life he left behind in Britain. Cripps' consideration of his position, and exploration of the notion of belonging — to a people, a land, a family and a love — illuminate both his life and the social history of Rhodesia/Zimbabwe and contextualise the troubled modern

Zimbabwe that Sheers experiences. Almost a hundred years before Sheers' visit, the missionary Cripps identified the problem of land and land ownership. At first, this awareness was prompted by his experience as a chaplain in East Africa during World War One when, as he witnessed men die while defending a line on a map, he saw the importance of ownership and belonging. On his return from that conflict, issues of land came to the fore through the plans of the British South Africa Company, which sought to reduce the million acres assigned to Black Africans. Cripps' recognition of the injustice of the amount of land assigned to the Africans (to work, but not own) by an institution that laid claim to territory that was not theirs to allocate, foresees the 'land question' that was central to Zimbabwe's independence struggle and continues to plague the country today. The 'dust' of the title is both the dust of history that has obscured the colonial context of the contemporary situation and the pervading dust of the veldt.

Sheers offers us a post-colonial vision of Zimbabwe, one that draws attention to the overlooked pre-colonial history, such as the medieval ruins of Great Zimbabwe and indeed the Shona institutions and conventions that the missionaries sought to 'civilise'. We witness how Cripps faces, accepts and respects the culture of the people of Marunda Mashanu, combining their beliefs with his own faith. This is exemplified by his church, inspired by the medieval ruins, the hymns he wrote in Shona, and ultimately, his funeral, when he was honoured with the burial anthems of a Shona chief.

The breadth of research and testimony collected in the novel reveals the great influence of Cripps' work, and its enduring legacy. However, equally as significant throughout the novel are the dust-hidden stories that Sheers uncovers, and the consequent exploration of love, loss and belonging. SM

)) Arthur studied the water below him again. He had seen no border interrupt its continuity. He had seen nothing but the moonlight, mineral across its supple surface. He thought to himself how ridiculous it was to take a ruler and a pencil and dash a border though a lake. Like portioning the sky or claiming the stars. And how childlike to label one side of the lake German and the other British. Childlike and futile. The imbricated obsession to own, to possess. And yet that ruler and pencil laid over the lake was enough to send two thousand of them across her waters tonight, weighed down with ammunition and intent. **((** 179

Thomas, Dylan

Portrait of the Artist as a Young Dog

Wales' most famous literary export is in delightful form with this collection of short stories first published in 1940. Like Joyce's masterpiece *Portrait of the Artist as a Young Man*, which the title comically echoes, this collection is also strongly autobiographical. It traces the early influences of people and places on Thomas' boyhood, adolescence and early manhood, with most of the stories told in the first person, adding to their immediacy.

The collection moves, almost chronologically, from pre-adolescent play and comedic schoolboy experiences through to a more self-conscious adolescence with its awareness of growing sexual and creative forces. The first two stories, 'The Peaches' and 'A Visit to Grandpa's,' detail the boy's perspective on holidays spent in the rural Welsh-speaking west of his colourful relations, a world away from his ordinary existence in urban Swansea.

He is spoiled by his gentle auntie Annie, forced to be a one-man congregation for his practice-preacher cousin Gwilym and woken up by his grandfather's nocturnal equestrianism. This is a world of childhood innocence, of dreams and imagination: 'I was aware of me myself in the exact middle of a living story and my body was my adventure and my name'. ('The Peaches')

The majority of the stories, though, are set in and around Swansea (or 'Tawe' from the Welsh name for the city, Abertawe). It is a 'shabby, spreading town where everything was happening' and from which the budding writer takes his inspiration. Distinct from the earlier stories in which experience is illustrated through cherished innocence, later stories trace the awakening knowledge of sexuality, death and loss. From the curly-headed slip of a boy experiencing puppy love for Jean — 'Although I knew I loved her, I didn't like anything she said or did' to the more urgent and anxious infatuation with Lou: 'the enchantment shining like a single line of light between them'. The boy as witness in the tale of two-timer Arnold ('Patricia, Edith and Arnold') becomes the adolescent lover experiencing first hand the illusory nature of love.

These glimpses into adult life transform the child's vivid imagination and love of storytelling into a more mature vision. The stories portray the developing desire of the young writer to experience and articulate the whole of life as it takes place around him. The comfort and care of his innocent early years give way to a need to witness, and then participate in the world, including its darker fringes as 'a lonely nightwalker and a steady stander-at-corners'. ('Just like little Dogs') This curiosity leads to a position on the local rag, further exposing him to the underbelly of his town: 'He had no need of the dark interior world when Tawe pressed in upon him and the eccentric ordinary people came bursting and crawling, with noise and colours, out of their houses, out of the graceless buildings, the factories and avenues, the shining shops and blaspheming chapels, the terminuses and the meeting-halls, the falling alleys and brick lanes, from the arches and shelters and holes behind the hoarding, out of the common, wild intelligence of the town. ('One Warm Saturday')

Thomas' stories are rooted in the real life experiences of a bustling sea-port, holidays spent in the countryside and of a childhood influenced by the contrast and clash of languages and cultures. The prose marries lyrical simplicity and comic realism, capturing the wide-eyed innocence of a young boy and the wily experiences of the adolescent writer. Though without the sharp satirical bent of some of his later work about Wales, Thomas is clearly aware here of class difference, captured by the attempts at suave sophistication at the Café Royal where the 'broad vowels of the town were narrowed in, the rise and fall of the family accent caught and pressed'. ('Old Garbo')

The value of these stories is in Thomas' memorable and diverting poetic prose and the warmth and compassion extended to his characters by a clear-seeing eye, gently ironic rather than sarcastic. As one of his narrators puts it: 'I had more love in me than I could ever want or use'. SRR

)) 'Now you confess,' said Gwilym.

'What have I got to confess?'

'The worse thing you've done'.

I let Edgar Reynolds be whipped because I had taken his homework; I stole twelve books in three visits from the library, and threw them away in the park; I drank a cup of my water to see what it tasted like; I beat a dog with a stick so that it would roll over and lick my hand afterwards; I looked with Dan Jones through the keyhole while his maid had a bath; I cut my knee with a penknife, and put the blood on my handkerchief and said it had come out of my ears so that I could pretend I was ill and frighten my mother; I pulled my trousers down and showed Jack Williams; I saw Billy Jones beat a pigeon to death with a fire-shovel, and laughed and got sick; Cedric Williams and I broke into Mrs Samuels´ house and poured ink over the bedclothes.

I said: 'I haven't done anything bad'. **((** 15

Trezise, Rachel

In and Out of the Goldfish Bowl

In and Out of the Goldfish Bowl is a vision of the Rhondda Valley in the 1990s, as witnessed and experienced by a teenage girl, Rebecca Trigianni. An account of life in one of the most deprived communities of Western Europe, where the mines have closed, but life remains as dark as the pits and the humour as black as the coal. A place where marginally employed adults drink and fight until they pass out, and where their children look for escape in alcohol, class B drugs, crime and underage sex.

The novel is a confessional memoir of youth, but Rebecca's memories of family life serve as a metaphor for the experience of south Wales' post-industrial communities. Among the episodes of a childhood, Trezise weaves sociological facts of the period, recounting how in 1985 in the aftermath of the Miners' Strike, unemployment in the Rhondda Valley stood as high as sixty-five percent; for her family however, this was a good time as both her mother and stepfather remained employed. Rebecca's contented home life is short-lived, though, since her stepfather, Brian, is made redundant when the last mine in the valley closes. Although the family celebrate receiving a redundancy money pay-out, it soon becomes evident that the cheque is not a ticket to a life of leisure. Both parents turn to alcohol, which leads to domestic violence, and then to Rebecca's rape by Brian.

The goldfish bowl of the title, therefore, is the claustrophobic 'glass coffin' that Rebecca occupies after she is raped; detached, trapped and unable to tell of the terrible incident. It is from there that Rebecca observes the Rhondda, its towns, villages and council estates now like a sealed-off goldfish bowl where unemployed children follow unemployed parents into the dole queue. Trezise portrays a place left behind by the optimistic wave of 'Cool Britannia'; the Rhondda is full of memories of a productive past but has now fallen into stagnation. The novel shows the underside of the supposed new and empowered era for Wales — a disintegrating, and dependent community.

The distance between the overlooked Rhondda and the vision of a new Britain is best illustrated in the novel through music. The action is played out to a 'soundtrack' of Tom Jones, Dolly Parton, the Sex Pistols, Guns N' Roses, Hole, and the Manic Street Preachers rather than optimistic Brit-pop. It is the experience of running away to the midlands when only fourteen, and watching bands play Nottingham's Rock City nightclub that makes Rebecca aware of the small-mindedness of the inhabitants of the Rhondda. Her head-turning piercings and Doc Marten boots reveal her defiance, but also provide her with a shield as she is neglected by her mother — who favours holidaying with her boyfriend over caring for her daughter — almost to the point of abandonment. At fifteen, Rebecca is living on her own in a house that was her mother's, shoplifting for the food she needs and relying on Valium for comfort as she cannot afford to switch on the heating.

Trezise's gritty novel is a continuation — and updating — of the tradition of Welsh industrial writing, a form that blends harsh fiction with fact. Informed by life in the Welsh valleys, it tells of the legacy of the now closed industries, and of the survival instinct of those in the post-industrial communities left behind. SM

)] She stepped away and he fell flat on his back. I couldn't see the knife. My mother kept backing away towards me. Creeping gently, shaking, the back of her head getting closer to my face. When she was gone the realisation was overwhelming. It was much too much to think about and I stepped toward my father with a phrase I thought would orphan me. 'Curiosity killed the cat'… Orphanage couldn't be so bad. Could not be as horrible as the bread knife planted through the inside of his upper arm. **[(** 43

Williams, Charlotte

Sugar and Slate

Sugar and Slate contains many valuable lessons within its pages — and one of them is to be wary of labels. Labels like 'black', 'white', 'British', 'Welsh', 'West Indian', 'African', 'immigrant'. Even such apparently indisputable, 'factual' labels as these are shown to be politically charged, loaded with assumptions and full of contradictions. Then there are other labels, widely used in the recent past but now seen as offensive: terms like 'coloured' and 'half-caste', words all too familiar to Charlotte Williams when she was growing up in Llandudno, a faded Victorian seaside resort on the north Wales coast. And then, of course, there are yet harsher labels… Though rarely the victim of such highly unpleasant taunts (the Llandudno of the 1950s and 1960s was, after all, a most polite and genteel town), Williams spent her formative years struggling to escape the labels society had burdened her with and, more insidiously, inculcated with the prevailing racist mentality, the labels she had given herself. One of five daughters of a black father from Guyana and a white 'Cymraes' (Welsh-speaking Welshwoman), perhaps the acceptable term to describe Williams nowadays would be 'mixed-race'. Part memoir, part travelogue, part racial treatise, this is both her story and history.

Williams begins with reference to the spectre of Africa, which 'hung about me like a Welsh Not' — following a damning report on educational standards in Wales by English officials in the mid-nineteenth century, the speaking of Welsh in schools was prohibited and the 'Welsh Not', a plaque worn about the neck of any child caught speaking Welsh during school hours, was one humiliating means of enforcing this diktat. Though not an officially sanctioned or universally used deterrent, the 'Welsh Not' has nevertheless become a powerful emblem of the suppression of the Welsh language. For Williams it has both personal and national significance. Deprived of the language of her foremothers (Welsh) and the language of her forefathers (Creole), she speaks English, the language of the oppressor, the language of the slave owners. She is condemned to define her identity in negative terms: in Wales she is 'not white', in Africa and Guyana she is 'not black'. As she explains in her preface, she grew up feeling 'that somehow to be half Welsh and half Afro-Caribbean was always to be half of something but never quite anything whole at all'. The rest of the book is dedicated to her quest for this elusive sense of wholeness, for a sense of acceptance and of belonging — a quest to find her way home.

Appropriately enough for a narrative in which journeys, both physical and spiritual, play such a vital part, Williams' reminiscences are framed by a chance encounter with a fellow delayed passenger in the departure lounge at Piarco Airport in Trinidad. Always travelling but never arriving, she is a legal alien, trapped in limbo between two cultures, two worlds, a fitting symbol of a life spent in transit and in transition. But then can any of us truly say we know where we're going? Williams' is a highly personal and yet universal story about the need to make sense of our past in order to make sense of our present and she becomes a most engaging guide on a collective voyage of discovery. CP

)) I've been trying to remember when this all began but I can't. It sort of built up slowly. I used to chant 'Eeny meeny miney mo, catch a nigger by his toe' along with the rest of them. I never imagined that I was the Golly on the Robertson's jar or the Black Jack on the sweet wrapper. There was a playground song that I found a great comfort in.

If you're white you're alright

If you're brown stick around

If you're black git back, git back, git back.

I wasn't black, I was brown, peanut brown. Africa was black, not me. The song announced the order of things and it made me safe. **((** 43

Williams, John

Prince of Wales

The crime thriller, immensely popular as a genre, is not everybody's cup of tea (or should that be 'mug of java'). *Prince of Wales*, one of a series by Cardiff-based journalist John Williams, was published both separately and in a cheap omnibus edition alongside two similar works under the title *The Cardiff Trilogy*. It has, as well as the hard-bitten one-dimensional types that constitute a crime writer's vision of the criminal world, an interesting portrayal of the interlocking elites of the Welsh capital. Williams' Cardiff has, in his dark, cynical vision, 'micro celebs of the Welsh media', local authority and Welsh Assembly fixers, gangland henchmen and journalists all mix 'n matching in dire schemes for mutual enrichment.

Connoisseurs of Britain's decaying Victorian cities will nod sympathetically as, in pursuit of regeneration and development, a vapid commercial cloning colonises the venerable if seedy docks area, a process which is a constant subtext of the book. The 'Prince of Wales' of the book's title, for instance, refers not to our helicoptering eco-Prince, but to a former porn cinema now bowdlerised into a trendy drinking shed for the young and thirsty. Similarly, a rough old pub called 'The Custom House' that has served immemorially as street HQ for the pimps and prossies of the Tiger Bay dockland is closed down at the start of the book to make way for the new Cardiff Bay Waterside.

The book in fact centres on the life of a Tiger Bay pimp, mixed-race lesbian Bobby, who, despite her profiting from prostitution, is the only character to show any kind of moral sensibility, no doubt an indication of Williams' unsympathetic view of Cardiff's go-getting elite.

Within the limits of the chilling unreflexivity of his characters with their cynical, utterly quotidian worldview — living only for the next fix, 'trick', drink, flash car, property deal or news story —Williams gives us a good bit of accurate social and micro-geographical detail of an otherwise obscure side of urban life, albeit inserted into the cold prose sandwich of thriller writing. RK

)) Outside St Clair led the way to a vantage point where they could look across the bay. He pointed over towards the new development.

'What d'you reckon?' he asked.

Pete looked across the water. He could see the St David's Hotel, Techniquest and the Sports Cafe, hidden behind which he knew there was Mermaid Quay, with its half-dozen restaurants, bank and comedy club and so-called designer clothes shop. He didn't think anything much about it. He used to go down there with Viv and the kids now and again, for a walk on dead Sunday afternoons, the girls complaining at being dragged away from the TV, or occasionally a family dinner at Harry Ramsden's or the Sports Cafe. It was OK.

'It's OK,' he said.

'Yeah,' said St Clair, 'that's exactly what it is. Nice. Nice like OK. Nice like it'll do for a place to go and eat in the evening if you can't face going into town. Yeah, it's nice. How about individual, though? Would you say it was individual?'

Pete thought about it, visualised the Mermaid Quay restaurants, the Bar 38 and the Via Fossa, the flash Italian and the flash Chinese.

'No,' he said, 'I suppose not'.

'No,' said St Clair, 'you're dead right it's not. What it is is off-the-peg bloody global capitalism. It's the kit version of a waterfront development. Half the restaurants here you could find the same place in any decent-size city in the UK: same menu, same gormless eighteen-year-olds pretending to be waiters on four quid an hour. You know what I mean?' **((** 503–4

Williams, Raymond

Border Country

Raymond Williams is a writer better known for his work in literary and cultural studies than his fiction, but his often overlooked novels are nonetheless important and interesting. *Border Country*, Williams' first novel and part of a border trilogy, is the story of the experiences of Matthew Price, a London-based lecturer, on his return to his family home in Glynmawr in the Welsh Marches. His visit is prompted by his father's poor health, and his return home causes both characters to (re)consider aspects of their lives and their relationship. Their exploration of their shared memories — especially those of the 1926 General Strike — reveals both personal histories and the social history of mid-twentieth century Wales.

Borders are a central motif of this novel — it was completed at the end of the 1950s, a time when the boundaries between literary and cultural theory were becoming more permeable. *Border Country* itself can be seen as being on a boundary, standing between fiction, reality and theory — a literary experiment strongly influenced by Williams' own critical work. This is evident in the exploration here of the socialist movement — the accounts of the General Strike and the disagreements between Harry, Matthew's father, a railway signalman, and the local entrepreneur. *Border Country* also has near-autobiographical elements as Matthew Price's position as an intellectual with working-class roots echoes that of Williams himself. The novel examines the dilemma of such individuals: are they 'organic' (Marxist theorist Antonio Gramsci's term) intellectuals truly emerging from their own popular background, or are they exiles, outsiders who are distanced from the political influences of their past? The position presented by the novel is that the past of the intellectual undoubtedly influences their work, but that they must write of the present of their communities from a distance. The liminal position of exile-returned is reflected in the novel in a matter central to Matthew's identity — his name. He was registered by his father as Matthew Henry Price, despite his mother's wish that he be named William; thus, over time Will becomes his Welsh identity, Matthew his intellectual, professional and English name.

The other significant border concept that permeates the novel is that between Wales and England — both the physical border as defined by maps and the metaphoric and cultural differences between the two nations, illustrated by Matthew's experience. The importance of identity in the region is further emphasised as the Welsh Marches is a marginalised area of a marginalised nation. This, as well as Matthew's research on migration in the nineteenth century Welsh coalfield, is used by Williams to reveal how Welsh identity and social history are continually oscillating.

Although *Border Country* is a book preoccupied with the role of the intellectual, the nature of history, Welsh identity and social change, the novel is still an affecting and moving consideration of the relationship between father and son. It remains as a fascinating exploration of the space between the people we once were in Wales and the people we have become. SM

)) He sat down, trying to breathe easily. Above him on the compartment wall was the familiar map. Wales, in this drawing, looked more than ever like the head of a pig, with the ears up at Pwllheli, the eye at Aberdovey, and the long snout running out to Fishguard, with Pembroke dock for a mouth. Pig-headed Wales then, is it? And us at its throat. Stubborn, self-willed, blind, I'm leaving? Not really. Not altogether. Whatever it is, it goes with you and comes back with you. The lines on the map ran out into England, and he followed them'. **((** 388–89

English-language poetry from Wales

Until the twentieth century there was no real tradition of English-language poetry in Wales. Welsh literary history spanned more than a millennium but was exclusively produced in the Welsh language. The linguistic balance of the country changed forever post-1900 and the majority of Welsh people are now English speaking (the Welsh-speaking proportion runs between 20 and 30% depending on how it is calculated). It is not possible here to convey the wide variety of English-language poetry from the last hundred years in Wales. It has, though been a history of conflict and creative struggle, as the poet John Davies wrote, commenting on the predicament of English-language writers in Wales, 'Being anglo-anything is really tough'.

Although poets like W.H. Davies and Huw Menai achieved some success in the early part of the twentieth century, it was a young Swansea man who demanded the attention of the literary establishment in 1937 with his *The Map of Love*. Dylan Thomas remains the most well-known and best-loved Welsh poet for an international audience. Regarded by many as the quintessential bohemian poet, Thomas' early work showed influences from Surrealism and Symbolism. Lines from one of the most remarkable poems of this period demonstrate a concern with the development of his poetic voice: 'The force that through the green fuse drives the flower/ Drives my green age'.

Thomas, like many of this 'first flowering' generation of Anglo-Welsh writers moved to London where he made a reputation for himself as poet and philanderer. His success in both engendered the hostility of the conservative intellectuals of his homeland, then coming to terms with the cultural anxiety triggered by the new bilingualism. But Thomas, like all English-language writers from Wales, was nurtured by the creative tensions that arose from this situation. The editor Keidrych Rhys, an influential contemporary, put it thus 'though we write in English, we are rooted in Wales'.

Critics argue that Thomas' verse became more accessible following a long period of prose writing and broadcasting. In this golden age of radio the BBC was an important vehicle for writers and many Anglo-Welsh authors found a creative platform with the Welsh Home Service, some like Glyn Jones producing thrilling radio poetry and Thomas himself became a master of creative talks*. What is certain is that his early sensual lyricism was tempered by a heightened sense of place, no doubt strengthened by his return to Wales (the rural west), the Blitz having decimated the Swansea of his youth. Significantly, many of the post-war poems recollect the child of a bygone era. The beauty and innocence that Thomas attributed to his boyhood is stunningly captured in one of his most famous poems 'Fern Hill', a hymn to his past and lament for the lost world of the pre-war years:

Now as I was young and easy under the apple boughs

About the lilting house and happy as the grass was green,

The night above the dingle starry,

Time let me hail and climb

Golden in the heydays of his eyes

(from 'Fern Hill')

Thomas' almost sacramental treatment of the natural world places him in the important tradition of praise poetry that dominates Classical Welsh poetry. However he was not religious and he rarely demonstrated any interest in the literary heritage of his country.

In the same year that Thomas' first publication appeared, another (more orthodox) sacramental poet who did have a passion for the Welsh literary heritage published his epic of war 'In Parenthesis'. David Jones, a former infantryman, produced one of the most compelling portraits of the suffering endured by all sides during World War One. It is a unique contribution to the canon of war poetry as it lacks the didactism, nostalgia or moralising tone often associated with this genre. It is a Modernist masterpiece drawing upon Welsh myth and early epic poetry, Shakespeare and Mallory, the intricacies of the Latin liturgy and the everyday language of the soldiers with whom he served. Daily hardships suffered are juxtaposed with eternal themes of existence, death and warfare through the ages. This passage from 'In Parenthesis' provides in one small image — a scurrying rat — the scale and brutality, psychological impact and physical discomfort of the conflict:

You can hear the silence of it:

you can hear the rat of no-man's-land

rut out intricacies,

weasel-out his patient workings

scrut, scrut, scrut,

harrow-out earthly, trowel his cunning paw

(from 'In Parenthesis')

It is difficult to categorise this work, part poetry, part prose, part 'shape in words' as Jones himself termed it. And the man too is elusive of definition. A painter and a poet with Protestant roots but a Catholic convert, a Londoner whose affiliation with his Welsh roots, traditions and language gave all his work unity and focus, Jones is often considered difficult and inaccessible but his reputation amongst fellow poets has never wavered.

Of the first generation of English-language poets to emerge from Wales one of the most popular and committed, as defined by T.S. Eliot's 'definite ethical and theological standpoint', was ex-miner Idris Davies. His poetry is a moving tribute to a particular community (the Rhumney valley) that suffered greatly during the General Strike of 1926 and the Depression. Fittingly Eliot was his publisher and would write after his death: 'his poems… are the best poetic document I know about a particular epoch in a particular place'. Though not a craftsman in the league of David Jones or Dylan Thomas, the poems show such sincerity and passion they continue to be read and appreciated today:

O that my passion would fuse

The valleys I love to flame,

The valleys of decent homes

Threatened by shadows of shame.

(from 'The Angry Summer')

The 1930s and 1940s saw the emergence of several important poetic voices in Wales that reacted against the social role of the artist and Eric Gill's mantra 'All Art is Propaganda' in favour of more imagistic, experimental poetry. Sometimes grouped together as the new or neo Romantics, poets like Alun Lewis, Vernon Watkins and Lynette Roberts forged a different poetic identity. The radical literary journal *Wales* featured these, and other, important voices like T.H. Jones and Nigel Heseltine writing at the time. Of these poets, perhaps the most important was Lynette Roberts, the Argentinean-born Welshwoman whose poetry is a remarkable record of the female response to an age riven by war:

A curlew hovers and haunts the room

On bare boards creak its filleted feet:

For freedom intones four notes of doom,

Crept, slept, wept, kept, under aerial gloom:

With Europe restless in his wing beat,

A curlew hovers and haunts the room

(from 'The Curlew')

The war silenced some of these voices for good and later the dominance of the Movement poets created a literary climate uncongenial for this type of work. During the post-war period a new and distinctive voice emerged, a poet who would become Wales' most important and uncompromising writer: R.S. Thomas. He introduced his archetypal Welsh peasant as:

Iago Prytherch his name, though, be it allowed,

Just an ordinary man of the bald Welsh hills,

Who pens a few sheep in a gap of cloud.

(from 'A Peasant')

The naturalness of his style and the freshness with which he approached the portrayal of the isolated hill communities where he was an Anglican vicar marked him out for early critical acclaim. Thomas went on to be one of the great metaphysical poets of the age, producing a body of work that unremittingly probes modern existence. He also applied his peculiar brand of belligerent questioning to his other great obsession, the 'matter of Wales'. No-one was left unscathed, as the following illustrates, and the Welsh were as likely targets as the English:

Where can I go, then, from the smell

Of decay, from the putrefying of a dead

Nation? I have walked the shore

For an hour and seen the English

Scavenging among the remains

Of our culture, covering the sand

Like the tide and, with the roughness

Of the tide, elbowing our language

Into the grave that we have dug for it.

This comes from a poem called 'Reservoirs', in allusion to the drowning of the Tryweryn valley in north Wales to supply water for Liverpool. The displaced community of the valley was Welsh-speaking Capel Celyn and it became a symbol of Britain's indifference to the destruction of rural Wales' way of life. The submersion of Capel Celyn inspired Saunders Lewis' (the most important Welsh intellectual of the twentieth century) to make his radio broadcast 'Tynged yr Iaith' (The Fate of the Language) in 1962. He categorically stated that Welsh would not survive the century's end without Herculean endeavour on the part of the people themselves**. Lewis' call galvanised a generation, creating a movement of civil disobedience that would ultimately bring official status for the language. Welsh-speaking creative artists were joined by a body of English-language writers whose commitment to safeguarding the Welsh language and Welsh cultural identity dominated their work. Tony Conran (an enthusiastic translator of Welsh-language literature) and Meic Stephens, activist and editor, were joined by poets like John Tripp and Harri Webb as voices of the 'second flowering' of Anglo-Welsh writing. Webb's 'Ode to the Severn Bridge'*** is indicative of his preoccupation with what he perceived as the inequality marking all areas of Welsh life:

Two lands at last connected

Across the waters wide,

And all the tolls collected

On the English side.

(from 'Ode to the Severn Bridge')

The politically charged 1960s and 1970s produced some interesting creative responses. Many writers felt compelled to take up Lewis' call to arms whilst others, most notably Leslie Norris, John Ormond and Dannie Abse, did not agree with the political engagement of their compatriots and their concern with craft above cause was an important counterbalance during this period. Abse's 'Return to Cardiff' illuminates his own perspective of place and provides a glimpse of his preoccupation with memory — real and imagined — and the temporal shifts that define our conception of the past:

No sooner than I'd arrived the other Cardiff gone,

smoke in the memory, these but tinned resemblances

where the boy I was not and the man I am not

met, hesitated, left double footsteps, then walked on.

(from 'Return to Cardiff')

The failed referendum of 1979 when Wales voted against devolution silenced many of the more militant nationalist voices. The new poetics that emerged emphasised the importance of broader issues and a growing internationalism that included a concern with green issues and the post-industrial landscape. Poetic voices as diverse as Mike Jenkins, Stephen Knight, Nigel Jenkins, Duncan Bush, Peter Finch, John Barnie, Tony Curtis and Robert Minhinnick matured at this time. And the last thirty years or so have also seen the rise of a professional body of critics, academic research on, and state funding for, English-language poetry in Wales. We now have healthy cross-cultural exchanges between English- and Welsh-language poetry, begun in the mid-1960s by Conran, Webb and Stephens and since developed in bilingual collections, translations and mutual critical appreciation.

A significant development of the recent past has been the rise of Welsh women's poetry in English. We can only glimpse here the remarkable body of work produced by poets like Gillian Clarke (the outstanding voice of this period), Sheenagh Pughe, Hilary Llewellyn-Williams and Ruth Bidgood. All share a sense of belonging and place firmly rooted in the landscape but with a desire to retrieve lost identity and forge new space in a largely patriarchal frame, well expressed by Llewellyn-Williams:

Something found only by digging, a glow in the dirt,

in the forest floor. Under rocks, under roots, what my heart

needs, what my soul feeds on. I will turn every stone

on earth, until I find what I'm looking for.

(from 'Ursa')

With the exception of already established male writers and a few outstanding new talents like Owen Sheers, the contemporary scene is dominated by women poets. Pascal Petit, Samantha Wynne Rhydderch, Sarah Corbett, Anna Wigley, Zoe Skoulding, Rhian Sadaat, Kathryn Gray, Deryn Rees-Jones and Gwyneth Lewis make for an impressive list.**** Gwyneth Lewis is, perhaps, the perfect embodiment of a confident bilingualism that welcomes the presence and creative opportunities of living with two languages. Lewis, an acclaimed modern poet, writes in both languages and was Wales' first National Poet. She covers the linguistic terrain without taking sides, her verse is not political but is knowing in a way that comes from intimacy with both cultures. Her poetry forms a fitting tribute to the vibrancy and diversity of contemporary English-language poetry from Wales. The following comes from her collection *Keeping Mum* (2003) and is a simple and powerful evocation of what it means to be a poet between two languages and how it feels to bear witness to an endangered linguistic inheritance:

'Aphasia'

I ask for hammer but am given 'spade',

Feel like some 'tea' but order 'orangeade'

by mistake. I specify 'velvet' but am given 'silk'

in a colour I don't even like

but I take it, pretend. Someone's cut the string

between each word and its matching thing,

so my mind's a junk shop of where i've been.

I'll never know now what I really mean.

(from *Keeping Mum*)

S.Rhian Reynolds

*'The Dream of Jake Hopkins' was broadcast in the exceptional Radio Odes series produced by Aneirin Talfan Davies for the Welsh Home Service. Other contributors included John Ormond and R.S. Thomas whose narrative poem 'The Minister' was an instant success.

**'The political tradition of the centuries, the whole economic tendency of the present age, are against the survival of the Welsh language. Nothing can change that except determination, will, struggle, sacrifice, effort'. Translated from 'Tynged yr Iaith'.

***The Severn Bridge links England and Wales across the river Severn in south Wales.

****Four of whom are included on the prestigious list of the twenty most vibrant British Next Generation poets.

EDITORS and CONTRIBUTORS

RK Ray Keenoy is the founding editor of the *Babel Guides* series to fiction in translation and oversees the work of Boulevard Books, a publishing house specialising in world literature. He holds a BA in Social Anthropology and Linguistics from University College London and an MA in Yiddish Language and Literature from the School of Oriental and African Studies in London.

SRR S.Rhian Reynolds is the editor of *A Bibliography of Welsh Literature in English Translation* (University of Wales Press, 2005). She completed her PhD at the Swansea University's CREW (Centre for Research into the English Literature and Language of Wales) in 2001 on the life and work of Aneirin Talfan Davies. She has worked in research in bilingual education, media and community development and is currently working as a research editor in Barcelona.

Sioned Puw Rowlands directs Wales Literature Exchange which promotes literary exchange between Wales and the world through translation. She is a Founding Editorial Director of *Transcript*, the online review for books and writing in Europe. Her publications include a collection of short stories, a book of interviews with Welsh authors and a critical study on minority aesthetics and the essay.

WA Will Atkins is a freelance editor, writer and reviewer living in Cardiff. Formerly he was Assistant Editor of the journal *Poetry Wales*, and Fiction Editor at one of Wales' leading literary publishers, Seren.

AB Angharad Brown read English at Oxford and subsequently worked at the Bodleian Library, before qualifying as a librarian and working for the Welsh Books Council. She is currently passing on her passion for literature and storytelling to her two young sons, and in the Welsh and English playgroups she runs. She translates and transcribes in her spare time.

FfD Fflur Dafydd is a fiction writer who writes in both Welsh and English. She is the author of three novels: *Lliwiau Liw Nos* (Y Lolfa, 2005), *Atyniad* (Y Lolfa, 2006) and *Twenty Thousand Saints* (Alcemi, 2008), and currently lectures in creative writing at Swansea University.

GD Gwen Davies is a fiction editor and founder of the fiction imprint Alcemi. She is the translator of Caryl Lewis' *Martha Jac a Sianco* (*Martha, Jack and Shanco*, Parthian 2007), and the co-translator of Robin Llywelyn's *Seren Wen ar Gefndir Gwyn* (*White Star*, Parthian, 2003). She grew up in a Welsh-speaking family in West Yorkshire, but has now spent most of her life in Wales.

DJ Diarmuid Johnson is visiting Professor of Celtic Languages and Literature at IFA, Adam Mickiewicz University, Poznan, Poland. He is author of *Súil Saoir* (CIC), a collection of poems in Gaelic, co-author of a French-language translation of poems by Dafydd ap Gwilym (Wodan Press), and translator into Gaelic of *Sarah Arall* by Aled Islwyn (CIC). His translation of Robin Llwelyn's short stories *Y Dŵr Mawr Llwyd (Big Grey Water)* is published by Parthian.

SPJ Sara Penrhyn Jones is an award-winning documentary maker based in Aberystwyth. She has also worked to promote Welsh literature internationally in her previous position as Project Officer with Welsh Literature Abroad. Currently on the board of *New Welsh Review*, she is writing a novel for teenagers.

CL-M Ceridwen Lloyd-Morgan was brought up in a Welsh-speaking community in north-west Wales. She studied languages and literature in Oxford and Poitiers and was on the staff of the National Library of Wales in Aberystwyth. She has lectured and published widely on the literature and visual arts of Wales and is currently Honorary Research Fellow in the School of Welsh, Cardiff University.

SM Sarah Morse is currently completing an MA dissertation on the historic and bardic nationalisms of R.S. Thomas at the Swansea University's CREW (Centre for Research into the English Literature and Language of Wales). She works in the School of Creative Arts and Humanities at Trinity College Carmarthen.

CP Claire Powell holds an MA in Modern Welsh Writing in English and a PhD in experimental poetry. She has worked for the University of Wales Press, Swansea University and, most recently, Swansea Institute. She has published widely on Welsh writing in English, Welsh popular culture and contemporary poetry and is a regular contributor to the literary periodicals of Wales.

HR Harri Roberts is a former doctoral student of the University of Glamorgan. His doctoral thesis, 'Embodying Identity: Representations of the Body in Welsh Writing in English', examined the imaging of the body in Wales's English-language literature and its significance in terms of the constructing (and contesting) of Welsh identity. Harri has published articles on Welsh literature and culture in the journal *Welsh Writing in English* and the online *North American Journal of Welsh Studies*, and is a regular contributor to the literary magazine *New Welsh Review*.

JR John Rowlands was brought up in rural Wales, and educated at local schools, then Bangor University and the University of Oxford. He pursued an academic career, retiring from the post of Professor of Welsh at Aberystwyth University. He has published seven novels in Welsh, and several critical studies of Welsh literature. He edited *The Bloodaxe Book of Modern Welsh Poetry* with Menna Elfyn.

GS Gareth Stanton has a PhD in anthropology and conducted fieldwork in North Africa and Spain. He is currently Head of the Department of Media and Communications at Goldsmiths, University of London. His recent work on world cinema has looked closely at Welsh cinema in particular.

Database of Welsh-language Fiction in English Translation

This database lists fiction – novels, short-story collections and anthologies – translated into English from the 1940s to the present. For convenience, anthologies are generally listed under 'Anthology'.

Record details:

AUTHOR SURNAME Author First Name
English Title (Year published)
Original Title (Year published)
Translator
Publisher Place of Publication **PAGES**

Notes:

This database includes information taken from the bwlet.net online database of Welsh literature in translation and the publication *A Bibliography of Welsh Literature in English Translation* (2005), edited by S.Rhian Reynolds. The editors of the *Babel Guide* are grateful for their help in sharing their data.

In-print Welsh interest books are readily available from gwales.com as well as bookshops.

ANTHOLOGY

Tony Curtis and Siân James (eds.)

Love from Wales (1991, 2005)
Seren, Bridgend 175

ANTHOLOGY

James A. Davies (ed.)

A Swansea Anthology (1996, 2006)

Seren, Bridgend 205

ANTHOLOGY

George Ewart Evans (ed.)

Welsh Short Stories (1959)
Faber & Faber, London 288

ANTHOLOGY

Gwyn Jones (ed.)

Welsh Short Stories (1937)
Faber and Faber, London 491

ANTHOLOGY

Gwyn Jones (ed.)

Welsh Short Stories (1956)
Oxford University Press, London 330

ANTHOLOGY

Gwyn Jones & Islwyn Ffowc Elis (eds.)

Twenty-five Welsh Short Stories (1971)
Oxford University Press, London 239

ANTHOLOGY

Gwyn Jones & Islwyn Ffowc Elis (eds.)

Classic Welsh Short Stories (1992)

first pub (1971) as Twenty-five Welsh Short Stories
Oxford University Press, London 239

ANTHOLOGY

Alun Richards (ed.)

The New Penguin Book of Welsh Short Stories (1993)
Viking, London 400

ANTHOLOGY

Alun Richards (ed.)

The Penguin Book of Welsh Short Stories (1976)
Penguin Books,London 358

ANTHOLOGY

Meic Stephens (ed. & tr.)

A White Afternoon & Other Stories (1998)
Meic Stephens

Parthian, Cardiff 243

ANTHOLOGY

Meic Stephens (ed.)

A Cardiff Anthology (1987, 1996)
Seren, Bridgend 197

ANTHOLOGY

Meic Stephens (ed. & tr.)

Illuminations: an Anthology of Welsh Short Prose (1998)
Welsh Academic Press, Cardiff 237

ANTHOLOGY

The Literary Review

Re-Imagining Wales

(2001) V44 n2
http://findarticles.com/p/articles/mi_m2078/is_2_44
NJ: Fairleigh Dickinson University, NJ 396

DAVIES E. Tegla

The Master of Pen y Bryn (1975)
Gwr Pen y Bryn (1923)
Nina Watkins
Christopher Davies, Llandybie 169

EAMES Marion

Fair Wilderness (1976)
Y Rhandir Mwyn (1972)
Elin Garlick with the author
Christopher Davies, Swansea 257

EAMES Marion

Fair Wilderness (1987)
Y Rhandir Mwyn (1972)
Elin Garlick with the author
Corgi, London 239

EAMES Marion

The Golden Road (1990)
I Hela Cnau (1978)
translated by author
Gwasg Gomer, Llandysul 234

EAMES Marion

The Secret Room (1975)
Y Stafell Ddirgel (1969)
Margaret Phillips with author
Christopher Davies, Swansea 186

EAMES Marion

The Secret Room (1995)
Y Stafell Ddirgel (1969)
Margaret Phillips with author
Gwasg Gomer, Llandysul 181

EDWARDS Sonia

White Tree (2006)
Y Goeden Wen (2001)
Sonia Edwards
Parthian, Cardiff 96

EDWARDS Sonia

A White Veil for Tomorrow (2001)
Rhwng Noson Wen a Phlygain (1999)
Sonia Edwards
Parthian, Cardiff 84

ELIS Islwyn Ffowc

Return to Lleifior (1999)
Yn Ôl i Leifior (1956)
Meic Stephens
Gwasg Gomer, Llandysul 301

ELIS Islwyn Ffowc

Shadow of the Sickle (1998)
Cysgod y Cryman (1953)
Meic Stephens
Gwasg Gomer, Llandysul 263

GRUFFYDD W.J.

The Years of the Locust (1976)
Hen Atgofion (1936)
D.Myrddin Lloyd
Gwasg Gomer, Llandysul 207

HUGHES T.Rowland

Out of their Night (1954)
Chwalfa (1946)
Richard Ruck
Gwasg Aberystwyth, Aberystwyth 265

HUGHES T.Rowland

Joseph of Arimathea (1961)
Yr Ogof (1945)
Richard Ruck
Gwasg Aberystwyth, Aberystwyth 250

HUGHES T.Rowland

The Beginning (1969)
Y Cychwyn (1947)
Richard Ruck
Gwasg Gomer, Llandysul 252

HUGHES T.Rowland

From Hand to Hand (1950)
O Law i Law (1943)
Richard Ruck
Methuen, London 198

HUGHES T.Rowland

William Jones (1953)
William Jones (1944)
Richard Ruck
Gwasg Aberystwyth, Aberystwyth 298

JONES John Gwilyn

The Plum Tree and Other Short Prose (2004)
Y Goeden Eirin (1946)
Meic Stephens
Seren, Bridgend 148

JONES R.Gerallt

Triptych: a portrait, in three parts, of Everyman (parallel text edition) (2001)
Triptych : neu bortread, mewn tair rhan, o Bobun (1977)
Jones, R.Gerallt
Gwasg Gomer, Llandysul 172

JONES Harri Pritchard

Corner People (1991)
n/a
Author, Harri Webb
Gwasg Gomer, Llandysul 97

JONES Jennie

Tomos the Islandman (parallel text) (1999)
Tomos o Enlli (1964)
Gwen Robson. illustrations by Kim Atkinson
Gwasg Carreg Gwalch, Llanrwst 112

JONES Dyfed Glyn

Albert Regina Jones (1975)
Albert Regina Jones (1973)

Dyfed Glyn Jones
Christopher Davies, Swansea 150

LEWIS Saunders

Monica (1997)
Monica (1930)
Meic Stephens
Seren, Bridgend 120

LEWIS Saunders

Plays vol. 1: The Vow, The Woman Made of Flowers, The King of England's Daughter (1985)
Joseph P. Clancy
Christopher Davies, Llandybie 154

LEWIS Saunders

Plays vol. 1: The Vow, The Woman Made of Flowers, The King of England's Daughter (2002)
Joseph P. Clancy
Gwasg Dinefwr, Llandybie 154

LEWIS Saunders

Plays vol. 2: Have a Cigarette? Treason, Esther (1985)
Joseph P. Clancy
Christopher Davies, Llandybie 196

LEWIS Saunders

Plays vol. 2: Have a Cigarette? Treason, Esther (2002)
Joseph P. Clancy
Gwasg Dinefwr, Llandybie 187

LEWIS Saunders

Plays vol. 3: Excelsior, Academic Affairs, Tomorrow's Wales, On the Train (1985)
Joseph P. Clancy
Christopher Davies, Swansea 196

LEWIS Saunders

Plays vol. 3: Excelsior, Academic Affairs, Tomorrow's Wales, On the Train (2002)
Joseph P. Clancy
Gwasg Dinefwr, Llandybie 196

LEWIS Saunders

Plays vol. 4: The Daughter of Gwern Hywel, The

Condemned Cell, The Two Marriages of Ann Thomas ((1986)
Joseph P. Clancy
Christopher Davies, Swansea 133

LEWIS Saunders

Plays vol. 4: The Daughter of Gwern Hywel, The Condemned Cell, The Two Marriages of Ann Thomas (2002)   Joseph P. Clancy
Gwasg Dinefwr, Llandybie 133

LLYWELYN Robin

From Empty Harbour to White Ocean (1996)
O'r Harbwr Gwag i'r Cefnfor Gwyn (1994)
Robin Llywelyn
Parthian, Cardiff 157

LLYWELYN Robin

White Star (2004)
Seren Wen ar Gefndir Gwyn (1992)
Llywelyn, Robin
Parthian, Cardiff 129

MORGAN Mihangel

Melog (2005)
Melog (1997)
Christopher Meredith
Seren, Bridgend 240

OWEN Daniel

Gwen Tomos (1963)
Gwen Tomos (1894)
Harries, Edward R. & Williams, T.Ceiriog
Hughes & Son, Wrecsam 222

PRICHARD Caradog

Full moon (1973)
Un Nos Ola Leuad (1961)
Menna Gallie
Hodder & Stoughton, London 192

PRICHARD Caradog

One Moonlit Night (1995)
Un Nos Ola Leuad (1961)
Philip Mitchell
Canongate, Edinburgh 176

PRICHARD Caradog

One Moonlit Night (parallel text) (1999)
Un Nos Ola Leuad (1961)
Philip Mitchell
Penguin, London 336

ROBERTS Kate

The Awakening (2006)
Y Byw sy'n Cysgu (1956)
Siân James
Seren, Bridgend 229

ROBERTS Kate

Feet in Chains (1977)
Traed Mewn Cyffion (1936)
Walters, Idwal & Jones, John Idris
John Jones, Cardiff 133

ROBERTS Kate

Feet in Chains (1980)
Traed Mewn Cyffion (1936)
John Idris Jones
Corgi, London 159

ROBERTS Kate

Feet in Chains (2002)
Traed Mewn Cyffion (1936)
John Idris Jones
Seren, Bridgend 174

ROBERTS Kate

The Living Sleep (1976)
Y Byw sy'n Cysgu (1956)
Wyn Griffith
John Jones, Cardiff (195

ROBERTS Kate

The Living Sleep (1981)
Y Byw sy'n Cysgu (1956)
Wyn Griffith
Corgi, London 203

ROBERTS Kate

One Bright Morning (2008)
Tegwych y Bore (1967)
Gillian Clarke
Gwasg Gomer, Llandysul 214

ROBERTS Kate

A Summer Day and other stories (1946)
Dafydd Jenkins and others
Penmark Press, Cardiff 121

ROBERTS Kate

Sun and Storm and Other Stories (2000)
Haul a Drycin (1981)
Carolyn Watcyn
Gee & Son, Denbigh 65

ROBERTS Kate

Tea in the Heather (1968, 1997)
Te yn y grug (1959)
Wyn Griffith
John Jones, Rhuthun 88

ROBERTS Kate

Tea in the Heather (2002)
Te yn y Grug (1959)
Wyn Griffith
Seren, Bridgend 85

ROBERTS Kate

Two Old Men and Other Stories (1981)
Stephens, Elan Closs & Griffith, Wyn
illustrated by Kyffin Williams
Gwasg Gregynog, Drenewydd 80

ROBERTS Kate

The World of Kate Roberts: selected stories (1991)
Joseph P. Clancy
Temple Univ. Press, PA 372

ROBERTS Kate

The White Road (parallel text) (2009)
Y Lôn Wen (1960)
Gillian Clarke
Gwasg Gomer, Llandysul 320

ROBERTS Wiliam Owen

Pestilence (1991)
Y Pla (1987)
Elisabeth Roberts
Hamish Hamilton, London 200

ROBERTS Wiliam Owen

Pestilence (1997)
Y Pla (1987)
Elisabeth Roberts
Seren, Bridgend 200

ROWLANDS John

A Taste of Apples (1966)
Ienctid yw 'Mhechod (1965)
Ruck, Richard
Library 33, London 127

ROWLANDS John

A Taste of Apples (1966)
Ienctid yw 'Mhechod (1965)
Ruck, Richard
Tandem Books, London 128

THOMAS R.S.

Autobiographies (1997)
Neb (1985)
Jason Walford Davies
J. M. Dent, London 192

THOMAS R.S.

Autobiographies (1998)
Neb (1985)
Jason Walford Davies
Phoenix, London 192

TOMOS Angharad

Twilight Song (Parallel text) (2004)
Si Hei Lwli (1991)
Elin ap Hywel
Gwasg Gomer, Llandysul 189

WILLIAMS Alun Llywelyn

The Light in the Gloom: Poems and Prose (1988)
Joseph Clancy
Gwasg Gee, Denbigh 210

WILLIAMS D.J.

The Old Farmhouse (1961)
Hen Dŷ Ffarm (1953)
Waldo Williams
Harrap, London 331

WILLIAMS D.J.

The Old Farmhouse (1987)
Hen Dŷ Ffarm (1953)
Waldo Williams
Golden Grove, Carmarthern 238

WILLIAMS D.J.

The Old Farmhouse (2001)
Hen Dŷ Ffarm (1953)
Waldo Williams
Gwasg Gomer, Llandysul 331